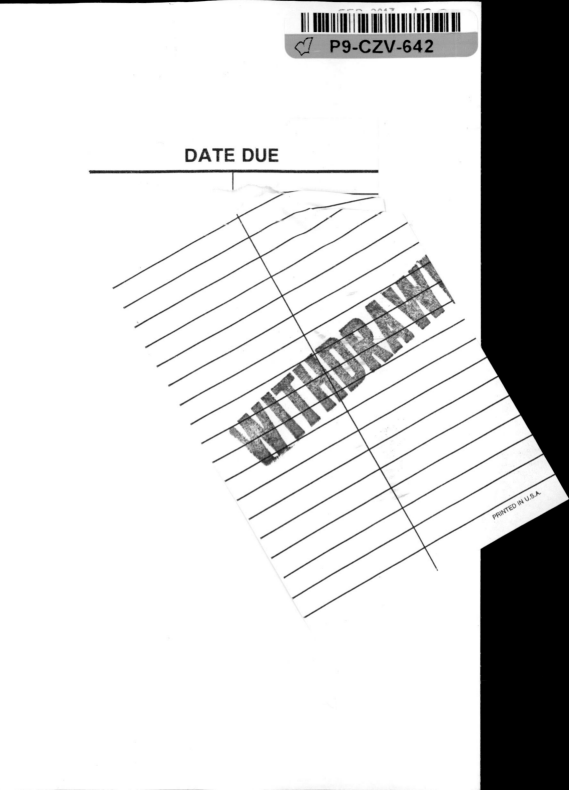

THE U.S. SENATE

ALSO BY SENATOR TOM DASCHLE

Getting It Done: How Obama and Congress Finally Broke the Stalemate to Make Way for Health Care Reform (with David Nather)

Critical: What We Can Do About the Health-Care Crisis (with Jeanne M. Lambrew and Scott S. Greenberger)

Like No Other Time: The 107th Congress and the Two Years That Changed America Forever (with Michael D'Orso)

ALSO BY CHARLES ROBBINS

The Accomplice: A Novel

Life Among the Cannibals: A Political Career, a Tea Party Uprising, and the End of Governing as We Know It (with Senator Arlen Specter)

Passion for Truth: From Finding JFK's Single Bullet to Questioning Anita Hill to Impeaching Clinton (with Senator Arlen Specter)

FUNDAMENTALS OF AMERICAN GOVERNMENT

★ ★ ★ ★ ★ ★ ★

THE U.S. SENATE

SENATOR TOM DASCHLE
and CHARLES ROBBINS

THOMAS DUNNE BOOKS
ST. MARTIN'S GRIFFIN
NEW YORK

THOMAS DUNNE BOOKS.
An imprint of St. Martin's Press.

THE U.S. SENATE. Copyright © 2013 by Tom Daschle and Charles Robbins. All rights reserved. Printed in the United States of America. For information, address St. Martin's Press, 175 Fifth Avenue, New York, N.Y. 10010.

www.thomasdunnebooks.com
www.stmartins.com

Design by Steven Seighman

Library of Congress Cataloging-in-Publication Data

Daschle, Thomas, 1947–
    The U.S. Senate : fundamentals of American government / Senator Tom Daschle and Charles Robbins.—1st ed.
        p. cm.
    Includes bibliographical references and index.
    ISBN 978-1-250-01122-0 (hardcover)
    ISBN 978-1-250-02755-9 (e-book)
    1. United States. Congress. Senate.   I. Robbins, Charles, author.   II. Title.
    JK1161.D375 2013
    328.73'071—dc23

                                                              2012038008

First Edition: January 2013

10 9 8 7 6 5 4 3 2 1

To my mother, Betty, who taught me to believe that my dreams and aspirations for public life were always within my reach.

—SENATOR TOM DASCHLE

For Charlotte and Victoria, who inspire faith in the next generation.

—CHARLES ROBBINS

☆ CONTENTS ☆

PART III: MOVING LEGISLATION

PART IV: BUDGETS, INVESTIGATIONS, SPECIAL SENATE FUNCTIONS

PART V: LIFE IN THE SENATE

PART VI: THE SENATE TODAY, AND TOMORROW

☆ ACKNOWLEDGMENTS ☆

Thanks, first, to Tom Dunne for an opportunity to convey and detail the Senate's key role in our democracy, and to contribute to his powerful "Fundamentals of American Government" series. Thanks, also, to Tom and to Katie Gilligan for their shrewd edits; to our agent, Victoria Skurnick, as always, for her expert guidance and support; and to Senate Historian Donald Ritchie for so generously sharing his insights, perspective, and institutional knowledge.

This book would not have been possible without the extraordinary efforts of my coauthor, Charles Robbins. His partnership in this project has been a source of true joy from start to finish.

PART
☆ 1 ☆

FOUNDATIONS

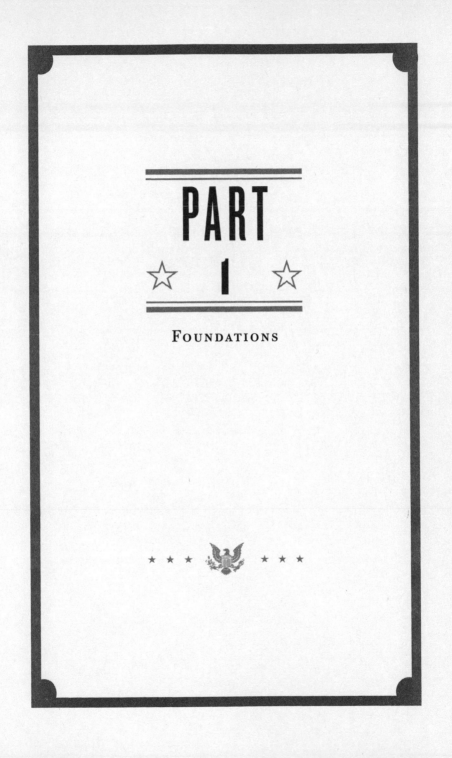

Every major issue makes its way to the U.S. Senate, from birth control to the death penalty, from declaring war to making peace. In addition to its role in passing laws, the Senate confirms or rejects the president's nominees for the Supreme Court, the Cabinet, and thousands of other posts; ratifies treaties; joins in declaring war; and convenes as an impeachment court. In our bicameral—or two-chamber—Congress, the Senate is "the saucer that cools the tea," a piece of lore going back to Washington and Jefferson about the Senate's role in tempering legislation from the sometimes heated House of Representatives.

As Ted Sorensen, President Kennedy's brilliant speechwriter, told me, "You make history every day."

Across America, since our country was founded, voters have chosen neighbors to represent them in the Senate, and sent them to Washington with great goals. But institutions, in many respects, are no better than the people who run them. The Senate reflects the country. We get what we vote for.

The Senate has seen great leaders as well as men who were not so great. In the Golden Age during the nineteenth century, the Great Triumvirate ruled—Daniel Webster, Henry Clay, and John C. Calhoun. In the 1950s, Joseph McCarthy's Communist witch hunts left a lasting stain on the Senate and the country.

A well-represented democracy and republic should have diversity that reflects its society, and the Senate still has a way to go. As late as the early 1950s, female staffers weren't allowed on the Senate floor. Today, several states are represented solely by women, and half the Senate staff is female. The Senate has also made progress on racial and ethnic inclusiveness.

An old adage holds that Congress was created by geniuses so it could be run by idiots. The Senate has withstood more than two hundred years of mistakes and missteps—even outright attempts to change the Framers' vision of the institution.

By putting the nation's good first, guided by history and individual conscience, the Senate helped hold our nation together and pull it back together after it ripped apart in the Civil War and to a degree during the civil rights battles. The Senate arguably saved the Judiciary and the Presidency by placing principle above politics in two presidential impeachments.

As Senate historian Donald Ritchie insists, you can't say the country grew naturally or organically; it grew because people set out to do something, and fought battles in Congress; in the Senate.

The Senate's framework has adapted to meet crises and environments that were unimaginable when it was created. What a testament to our forefathers' foresight, brilliance, and insight into the human spirit—both its dark and bright sides—that they could create such a resilient and adaptive system of government.

The question now is whether it is adaptive enough. Most Americans think the federal government is dysfunctional, unable to deal with our country's most pressing problems, including energy, climate, the budget, the economy, joblessness, education, health care, and infrastructure. As the United States has gone from independence to increasing economic and social integration with the rest of world, we need a level of leadership and competence in governance that we're not showing regularly these days.

The Senate is called both the World's Greatest Deliberative Body and the Most Exclusive Club. It's also said that the Senate is the only place in the country where somebody stands up to speak, nobody listens, and then everybody disagrees. All carry an element of truth. The Senate has always had partisanship, and some rancor and gridlock, too. In the old days, the Senate floor saw pulled pistols, a cane beating, and a punch in the jaw.

The Senate, at its core, is a complex web of relationships—a hundred men and women from different backgrounds, beliefs, points of view, experiences, and abilities, all thrown together to make the laws of the land. They all have their own obligations to both the nation as a whole and to their individual states and constituencies. The process and discipline of reasoned, rigorous debate shapes strong, sound legislation and policy. Confrontation with civility is exactly what our Founding Fathers had in mind. Sometimes we lose that civility, and that's where the problems begin.

Especially in today's challenging times, effective citizenship demands understanding American government, including the Senate. This book offers a firsthand guide to the Senate, with particular attention to such key elements as committees, rules, legislation, holds and filibusters, coalitions, vetoes and overrides, the federal budget process, oversight and investigations, nominations, impeachment, declaring war, and treaties—and on opportunities to serve.

Those opportunities begin early. High school students can serve as Senate pages, college students as interns, and recent graduates as staff. Many of them return in senior positions and increasingly, as I did, as House members and senators. The country needs engaged, informed citizens—you get what you vote for—and it needs great leaders.

☆ I. A CHAIN OF HISTORY ☆

When a newly elected member arrives in the Senate, he or she gets a number corresponding to that person's place in the line of all senators who have served since the body was created. As of this writing, 1,931 senators have served. Robert Morris and William Maclay of Pennsylvania—who grew to detest each other—got numbers one and two because their state was the first to elect its senators. The first group of twelve senators arrived at the same time, April 6, 1789. When I joined the Senate in 1987, I was both amazed and delighted at the number I was given: 1776, the year the American colonies declared independence from Britain.

From the moment a new senator first steps onto the Senate floor, most are powerfully aware that we are links in an extraordinary chain of history going back to the Founders, the heirs and guardians of a miracle. And that miracle is the ideal of the United States, which we embrace, and whose great freedoms we swear to protect.

Eight years after I arrived, the senators of my party elected me their Leader, and one of my strongest supporters and most loyal and dedicated friends, Dick Reiners, invited me to dinner back home in South Dakota. Dick, then in his eighties, was a farmer. Over meat and potatoes at Dick's farmhouse in Worthing, I asked him for advice. He paused and looked at me and said, "There are two things that I would hope for you. One is that you never forget where you came from. Come home. Remember us." Then he pointed to some photos on the wall that I recognized readily, of his grandchildren. He said, "You've held each one of those grandkids, as have I. Give them hope. Every day you walk onto the floor, give them hope."

We hugged, and I left. Hours later, in the middle of the night, I got a call that Dick had passed away.

I've never gotten better advice in all the years before or since, and it has stayed with me. From across America, since our country was founded, voters have chosen neighbors to represent them in the Senate, and sent them to Washington with great goals. A senator's challenge is to focus on those goals and not lose sight of them amid the daily bustle and battles. That can be particularly challenging in today's tough times.

One touchstone, in particular, helped me remember my purpose: the Senate Leader's desk, at the front of the chamber. The desks, made in 1819, each have an ink well and a snuff box. You pull open the drawer, and you see the names of all the Leaders carved in it, and other senators, all those who used the desk before you.

As they sit at those desks, senators take on the challenge to safeguard our freedom, the same challenge that American soldiers have met for more than two centuries, and for which more than a million men and women have given their lives in more than thirty wars.

I represented South Dakota, first in the House of Representatives and then in the Senate—the two bodies that comprise the U.S. Congress—and served my last ten years as Senate Democratic Leader, including stints as Minority Leader and Majority Leader, depending on which party held more seats. For twenty-six years, the people of South Dakota—and colleagues from across the country—allowed me to live my passion.

I was raised Catholic, and my Catholicism was a huge part of my life when I was young. For many, from ordained clergy to the millions who volunteer through faith-affiliated groups and activities, the church is a calling, a way of serving something beyond themselves, a way of helping others. I rode my bike to mass every morning before school, even in numbing South Dakota winters. For me, the one action that evokes many of the same sensations as walking into a church is stepping onto the Senate floor. The majesty, the richness, the history, and sometimes the hush of the Senate chamber are akin to that of a sacred place. It was my secular temple.[1]

It's a rare privilege to serve in the U.S. Senate. It's not easy to get there, or to stay there. Before you can try to realize your goals and visions, though, you have to convince your neighbors that you can best represent their views and interests in Washington. Alben Barkley, a Senate Majority Leader and later vice president, was asked what makes a great senator. "To be a great senator," Barkley replied, "first you have to get elected."

But in America, you don't have to be rich or connected or go to "the right schools" to win a Senate seat, or even become Majority Leader. You can come from a farm family in a small Midwestern state, and be the first in that family to graduate from college, like me. You just need to be thirty years old by the time you take office, a U.S. citizen for nine years, live in the state in which you run, and make the best case to your neighbors why they should send you to Washington.

Once you're in, the Senate itself—the Capitol, the chamber, your colleagues, the desks, the statues, the art, the history—should channel what Abraham Lincoln called the "better angels of our nature" and buttress you. Mike Mansfield, the great and longest-serving Senate Majority Leader, said, "What moved Senators yesterday still moves Senators today. We have the individual and collective strength of our predecessors . . ."[2]

2. MAKING HISTORY EVERY DAY

When I was a senator, Ted Sorensen, President Kennedy's brilliant speechwriter, told me, "You make history every day." He was right. Every major issue eventually makes its way to the U.S. Senate, from birth on abortion and contraception to death on assisted suicide and capital punishment, and everything in between. The Senate ratifies treaties; joins in declaring war; confirms or rejects the president's nominees for the Supreme Court, the Cabinet, and thousands of other posts; and convenes as an impeachment court.

I served in painful days for the Senate and the nation, challenging times of great potential consequence. As I said at the time, "Our responsibility . . . is to put the good of our Nation first, to be guided in these difficult days by two things only: our history and our own individual consciences."

That approach, that premium on history and conscience, allowed the Senate to play key roles in holding our nation together and pulling it back together after it ripped apart in the Civil War and to a degree during the civil rights battles, and in arguably saving the judiciary and the presidency by placing principle above politics in two presidential impeachments.

As Senate historian Donald Ritchie insists, you can't say the country grew naturally or organically; it grew because people set out to do something, and fought battles in Congress. "A lot of what we take for granted today was the result of long-term, major battles that resulted in the legislation." Ritchie recalled:

> When I came to Washington in the 1960s, you couldn't stand next to the Potomac River because it smelled so bad, and if you fell in, you needed to get a Tetanus shot, because it was an open sewer—all these little towns up in Maryland and Virginia were just dumping their sewage into it. Now, I go by the Potomac and I see crew teams, I see people fishing and kayaking in the river. And the river smells decent. It happened because they passed the Clean Water Act.[1]

Passed in its current form in 1977, the Clean Water Act regulates quality and discharges of pollutants into U.S. waters.

Ritchie also cited the Americans with Disabilities Act, a 1990 law that opens jobs, transportation, buildings, and communications to people with a disability, from blindness to deafness to activity-restricting diseases. That's why you see ramps on buildings, wheelchair lifts on buses, and TTY lines on phones. The legislation brought together a strange bipartisan (both Democratic and Republican) assortment of senators, Ritchie noted, with one thing in common—they all had relatives with disabilities. "They knew how awful it was, and they knew how hard it was to get public places to accommodate them."[2]

Senators also devote enormous effort to directly helping people cut through the red tape of federal bureaucracy, replacing a lost

Social Security check or enrolling a veteran for treatment or earned benefits. That "constituent service" in some ways offers the job's greatest reward. There's nothing like the thrill of a neighbor coming up and gushing that you saved his or her life.

George Mitchell was one of the most distinguished Majority Leaders in our nation's history, a former federal judge who later brokered the Northern Ireland "Good Friday" peace agreement, ending a three-decade civil war that claimed more than 3,200 lives. Through all of his accomplishments, the single most satisfying moment of Mitchell's public life occurred, he said, in a parking lot of Sonny Miller's restaurant in Bangor, Maine, when a burly man rushed up to him. Mitchell's first thought, he said, was that the man was going to hit him. Instead, the man hugged him and thanked him for saving his job, by saving a small paper mill in Maine. Tears were streaming down the man's face as he described how much Mitchell's actions had meant to him and to his family. For George, a son of immigrants who had worked his way through school as a janitor, it was a singular moment in a singular career.

☆ 3. POLITICAL PARTIES ☆

The Constitution does not mention political parties. James Madison, often called the Father of the Constitution, warned in "Federalist No. 10" of the evils of "faction." Still, our new country adopted England's structure of two competing parties. In the 1720s, the Whigs and Tories crossed the Atlantic. The Tories began as the "court party," later the loyalists. The two parties evolved into Federalists and Anti-Federalists and eventually into Democrats and Republicans.

Now, after two centuries, our two major political parties, the Democrats and Republicans, have shaped the U.S. political system at both the state and federal levels. They use devices such as filing fees and petitions to restrict ballot access to others, whom they dismiss as "third" and "fringe" parties.

Our two political parties are fundamental to American government and politics, and to the Senate. The Senate chamber itself, the sanctuary, has a center aisle that divides along party lines, spawning the phrase "crossing the aisle" when you work with somebody from the other party. Each party has its own "cloakroom," with a door into the Senate chamber. The political parties assign their members to committees and select their leaders, the Majority and Minority Leaders, who manage legislation on the floor.

Democrats and Republicans have different, competing philosophies. President Franklin Roosevelt offered as succinct a definition of the difference between liberals and conservatives—essentially, between Democrats and Republicans—that I've ever seen, a definition that is as accurate today as it was back then. Liberals, FDR said, believe that "as new conditions and problems arise beyond the power of men and women to meet as individuals, it becomes the duty of government itself to find new remedies with which to meet them." Conservatives, he said, believe that "there is no necessity for the government to step in." President Ronald Reagan, a conservative in office during the 1980s, liked to say that government is the problem, not the solution. That, even more than FDR's definition, sums up the difference between the Republican and Democratic ideologies that have evolved in the past thirty years, and the schism between the two views in American politics.

In 1991, as cochair of the Senate Democratic Policy Committee, I was tasked with crafting my party's agenda for the 102nd Congress, which would run the next two years, in FDR's spirit of government duty. I visited each Democratic office to survey senators' views and to collect ideas. Everybody I spoke with wanted health care reform at or near the top of our agenda. And so I helped launch an effort that would become a cornerstone of my career, and a cornerstone of two administrations.

☆ 4. BIPARTISANSHIP ☆

When I was first elected to Congress 1978, the Senate was "a bipartisan liberal institution," as Senate historian Ritchie described it. By bipartisan, he meant that Democrats and Republicans cooperated and compromised to achieve results. In a masterful portrait of the Senate in *The New Yorker* magazine, George Packer noted, "Every major initiative—voting rights, open housing, environmental law, campaign reform—enjoyed bipartisan support."[1]

Today, the Senate is a vastly different place. The Senate's modern, fractious era grew from the upheaval of the 1960s and 1970s. In his 1969 inaugural address, President Richard Nixon urged civility, as the Vietnam War and the counterculture revolutions raged: "We cannot learn from one another until we stop shouting at one another."

When I arrived in Washington in January 1979, the Senate had just begun its decline. Packer traced the slide to 1978.

The Senate's modern decline began in 1978, with the election of a new wave of anti-government conservatives, and accelerated as Republicans became the majority in 1981. . . . Liberal Republicans began to disappear, and as Southern Democrats died out they were replaced by conservative Republicans. Bipartisan coalitions on both wings of the Senate vanished.[2]

When the system works, senators can disagree without being disagreeable, as the saying goes. In a healthy democracy such as ours, it is not only the right, but the duty of the "opposition party" to fight for what it believes in. You hope to end up with principled compromise, to find common ground. Everett Dirksen, the great Senate Republican leader and namesake of a Senate office building, said, "I live by my principles and one of my principles is flexibility."

But sometimes there is sacred ground, and that's when you agree to disagree. It is out of the process and discipline of reasoned and rigorous debate that strong and sound legislation and policy are shaped. Such debate is at the heart of the system of government created by our Founding Fathers.

Some partisanship is healthy, organizing the Senate and cohering substantive agendas, and bringing a competition of ideas and philosophies, and national dialogs and debates. Republican Leader Bob Dole, invoking former Democratic Presidential candidate Adlai Stevenson, called principled partisanship the lifeblood of democracy.[3]

When most people think of the phrase "checks and balances," they think of the separate branches of our government—the presidency, Congress, federal and state governments, the judiciary. But the phrase also pinpoints a minority party's duty in the Senate—in the Democrats' case, when I was Minority Leader, to check and to balance, wherever we thought it necessary, the legislative intentions of the Republican Party and the Republican White

House. The Republicans pursued the same goal, through different means, during the Clinton presidency.

A political party has rarely achieved a big enough majority in the Senate to simply steamroll the minority to pass its legislation. Most recently, Democrats captured those numbers during the Great Depression, when they shepherded through New Deal legislation, the sweeping federal programs that helped lift America out of the depths of the financial crisis and carried us through World War II and beyond; and in the 1960s, when they passed Great Society programs, to attack poverty and encourage social justice.

In both those eras, Democrats also controlled the White House and the House. But even with such command—and certainly without it—legislation is far stronger and more appealing when it carries bipartisan support. Support from members of both parties muzzles partisan radio and TV talk-show hosts and "special interests," or advocacy groups, aligned with one side or the other. "Centrist" senators are more willing to support bipartisan bills. Like Blanche Lincoln, an Arkansas Democrat who wanted bipartisan support for the massive 2010 health care bill, at a time when she was facing reelection the next year in a state that had voted for the Republican Presidential nominee, Senator John McCain, by 20 percentage points over the Democratic nominee, then-Senator Barack Obama. The health care bill did not attract any Republican support, and Lincoln wound up casting a deciding vote for it and losing her election, though that vote was hardly the only cause. For the Senate's majority party, working with the minority party is essential. And so is working with today's opponents—who may become tomorrow's allies.

After the final vote of a tough battle, Senate Republican Leader Howard Baker routinely extended his hand to his main opponent. "This ritual is as natural as breathing here in the Senate," Baker later said, "and it is as important as anything that happens in Washington or in the country we serve, for that matter."[4]

The respect goes to the heart of the Senate, and back to its birth. In the Senate's Golden Age, the days of high oratory, the Great Triumvirate held sway—Senators Daniel Webster, Henry Clay, and John C. Calhoun. They sparred and debated and denounced each other. Toward the end of their time, Calhoun declared, "I don't like Henry Clay. He is a bad man, an imposter, a creator of wicked schemes. I wouldn't speak to him. But by God, I love him." In other words, Calhoun disagreed with Clay's views and found his proposals dangerous, but respected and admired Clay as a fellow master politician and senator.

In earlier eras, personal bonds used to unite senators. Common military service provided strong ties, with camaraderie flowing at Marine Corps, Navy, and Army breakfasts. In the 1970s, seven out of ten senators had served in the armed forces. Today, two of ten have. I served three years as an Air Force intelligence officer, and did form bonds over military service with Senate colleagues on both sides of the aisle, including John Kerry (D-Mass.), John McCain (R-Ariz.), Chuck Robb (D-Va.), Daniel Inouye (D-Hawaii), Bob Kerrey (D-Neb.), and Chuck Hagel (R-Neb.).

Apart from any military ties, I have made many good friends from the other side of the aisle, including former South Dakota Governor and Congressman Bill Janklow and Kansas Senator Bob Dole. I forged a good working relationship with Dole during the eighteen months when we were both Leaders, despite tough circumstances. Dole loves his party. That was always very clear to me. But there is something even more important to him than party, and that is principle.

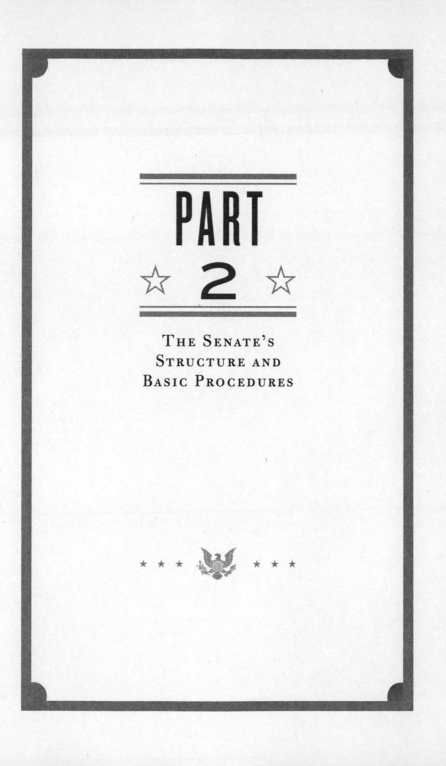

PART
☆ 2 ☆

THE SENATE'S
STRUCTURE AND
BASIC PROCEDURES

5. THE SYMBOL OF AMERICAN DEMOCRACY

The word "Congress" comes from the Latin for "coming together," where elected officials from throughout the country, each representing his or her own state and local interests, convene. Congressional sessions now begin early each January and run year-round, with periodic breaks, including a month-long August recess. Serving in the Senate used to be a seasonal, part-time job in the republic's early days and before air-conditioning made the sweltering D.C. summers bearable. Newspapers routinely carried items about senators summering in Europe. The new, full-time regimen began in 1934.

Our national legislature—both houses of Congress—and the other branches of federal government are all based in the nation's capital of Washington, D.C., formally The District of Columbia, a swath of land on the Potomac River donated by the State of Maryland and named after our nation's first president, George Washington. Federal government settled in "D.C." or "The District" at the turn of the nineteenth century, after brief stints in New York, Philadelphia, and Princeton, New Jersey.

The U.S. Capitol serves as Congress's base, and sits on a rolling hill, prompting the moniker "Capitol Hill" or simply "The Hill." One semiweekly newspaper that focuses on Congress calls itself *The Hill*.

The U.S. Capitol, the most recognizable symbol of American democracy, is a magnificent white colossus of marble and limestone capped by a painted cast-iron dome. The building rests at the hub of several boulevards, and offers a dazzling sight as you approach, either driving or strolling, maybe most strikingly when lit against the night sky. Lawmakers have said for generations that when the sight of the Capitol ceases to awe you, it's time to move on. I used to enjoy giving tours of the Capitol dome, taking my guests through narrow stairs, ladders, and landings, explaining the famous Constantino Brumidi mural in the dome ceiling, to the highest stone ring just below the Statute of Freedom.

If you ever get a chance to visit Washington, the U.S. Capitol is a must-see. I'm proud of my work to build the new Capitol Visitor Center. I was inspired by the underground visitors center in Austin, Texas. It was a long time in coming, with strong opposition from many. It has made the Capitol more secure and provided a vastly improved visitor experience, in addition to providing much-needed meeting and function room space. Jeri Thompson, who served as the Secretary of the Senate during my tenure as Majority Leader, was the real force behind getting this done.

The Capitol is a bustling office building, a national showplace and a museum, all in one. Busts of all the vice presidents, whose jobs included presiding over the Senate, loom larger than life. Many of those "veeps" or "VPs," such as Thomas Jefferson and Theodore Roosevelt, remain heroes for the ages. But some got into enormous trouble. Aaron Burr, Jefferson's vice president, killed Treasury Secretary Alexander Hamilton in a pistol duel and became a fugitive from justice. Burr amazingly was never convicted and actually came back to serve out his term as Senate president. Spiro Agnew, Richard Nixon's VP, resigned after pleading "no contest" to charges of unpaid taxes amid a bribery investigation. Then add more layers of history—in every room, momentous plans were shaped and events held.

To remind my fellow senators of our rich history, when it came time to decide the format for President Bill Clinton's impeachment trial in 1999, I pressed to hold the full-Senate meeting in the grand old Senate chamber, where giants including Daniel Webster, Henry Clay, and John Calhoun shaped this nation. But we'll get to that.

The Capitol houses both the House and Senate. The rotunda, in the center of the building, serves as the dividing point. Each side of the Capitol has a different feel, a different vibe, and even longtime members of one body can have trouble navigating the other side.

☆ 6. "THE HILL" ☆

While senators debate and vote in their large, majestic Capitol chamber, and often meet in the building's leadership and committee offices and reception rooms, they spend the bulk of their Washington work time in their private offices in one of three Senate office buildings. A network of underground trams connects those buildings to the Capitol, and a similar network connects the three House office buildings to the Capitol. A maze of basement corridors runs throughout the complex. You can travel from any House or Senate building to any other building on campus without ever stepping outdoors, if you know the route. But a wrong turn into a winding, unmarked corridor can easily add fifteen minutes to the trip.

Members moved into their current chamber in 1859, when the Senate grew to sixty-eight members as more states joined the union, and senators outgrew the grand old chamber they had used since 1810. Until the early twentieth century, senators' primary workspaces were their desks on the Senate floor.

In 1909, senators each took an office in the newly built Senate

Office Building—now the Russell Senate Office Building, in honor of Senator Richard Russell of Georgia. The neoclassical palace of white Vermont marble moved *The New York Times* to write, "Never in the history of the world was there such an office building." Harry Truman, first elected to the Senate in 1934, told constituents they could reach him by simply mailing "Truman, S.O.B., Washington." As the Senate and its staff kept growing, the Senate broke ground on a second office building. When that new building opened in 1958, the original building became "Old S.O.B." and the new one "New S.O.B." That new building is now known as the Dirksen Building, after Senator Everett Dirksen of Illinois.

During the 1970s, Senate staff more than doubled, forcing some aides to nearby commercial buildings. The Senate dug ground for a third office building, right next to Dirksen, to be named after ailing Senator Philip Hart of Michigan. The Hart Building budget tripled, and the structure came out, as some saw it, a stark, modern white box. When workers removed the plastic sheathing over the frame that had allowed winter construction, unveiling the finished building, Senator Daniel Patrick Moynihan of New York issued a "Sense of the Senate" resolution in May 1981, urging that the plastic cover be put back on. But other senators found the modern new Hart Building welcoming. I chose a personal office on the fifth floor of Hart, which served my staff and me very well.

In addition to at least one Capitol Hill office, each senator also has offices throughout his or her state. The number depends largely on the size of the state. A senator's Washington office generally houses the senator's chief of staff, legislative director, communications director and other senior managers, scheduler and executive assistant, press secretaries and legislative aides, and office administrators. The "state offices" back home generally house caseworkers, who help constituents cut through red tape in dealing with executive agencies, and other outreach staff, with the state director based in the main state office. Senators assemble their offices as they see fit, though, and no two are structured exactly alike. Senators also pay their aides as they see fit, covering salaries from the same overall budget that must also fund offices, travel, and other expenses, so there's also no uniform Senate pay scale. A Leader probably has double the staff of other senators, including floor staff, who oversee action in the chamber; and leadership staff, who tend the leadership committees and party caucuses.

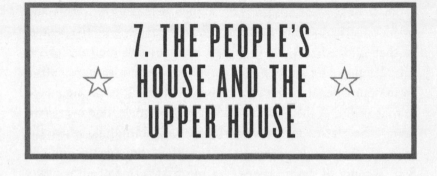

7. THE PEOPLE'S
☆ HOUSE AND THE ☆
UPPER HOUSE

Operationally as well as physically, the U.S. Congress is a "bicameral legislature," composed of two bodies, the Senate and the House. The two chambers operate as separate entities under one roof, each with its own leadership and rules. They refer to each other as "the other body." But neither can pass a law or allocate funds on its own. They must collaborate; each must pass legislation in exactly the same form to send to the president.

At the Constitutional Convention in 1787, the Founders wrestled with the structure of Congress, and created the Senate through what was essentially a political deal. The larger states wanted to set the number of representatives in each chamber of Congress proportionately according to the states' populations, arguing that more people deserved more representation. The smaller states wanted to set a fixed number of representatives from each state in each chamber, arguing that each state deserved an equal voice. A committee came up with the Great Compromise: proportional representation in the House and equality—two representatives each—in the Senate.

Members of the House serve two-year terms, so they're always in an election cycle. As soon as they're sworn in, they must begin their next campaign. House members' shorter terms and smaller districts, at least in theory, make them closer to the people. In that spirit, the House of Representatives is sometimes called "The People's House." Senators serve six-year terms, representing entire states. Senators serve in "classes," with their terms staggered so that a third of the Senate's seats come up for election every two years. The classes go back to the nation's founding, when the original senators drew lots to see whether they would join the first, second, or third classes, getting first terms of either two, four, or six years.

Originally, senators did not stand for election by popular vote. Instead, their individual state legislatures chose them. That changed in 1913, through the Seventeenth Amendment to the Constitution. The shift to direct election may have made senators closer to the voters, whom they now courted for support, but the change was driven largely to combat growing corruption. Some state legislators allegedly took bribes to vote for Senate candidates, while gridlock in statehouses left Senate seats vacant for an entire Congress. As America became an industrial power, some business leaders pressured state legislatures to vote for their candidate, and several got themselves elected to the Senate. Still, when senators went on the public ballot in 1914, voters reelected every incumbent running. The state legislatures, Ritchie noted, had not been far removed from public opinion.

If the House of Representatives is "The People's House," the Senate is "The Upper House." The expression goes back to the first Congress in New York's Federal Hall, when the Senate chamber was upstairs, above the House chamber. But the name has deeper meanings.

Some of the Founders envisioned the Senate as a preserve of

gentlemen. They proposed that senators should be unpaid, to attract wealthy aristocrats who could afford the time to do the job. The term "Senate" comes from the same root as "senile," referring to aging. The Constitution requires senators to be thirty years old by the time they take office. (Senators can be elected shy of their thirtieth birthdays, as some have, including Vice President Joe Biden, formerly a longtime senator from Delaware; they just have to be thirty by the time they're sworn in.) House members, by contrast, must be twenty-five by the time they are sworn in.

With the House, small, often politically homogenous congressional districts can elect more ideologues, and the House's stricter majority rule can lead to passage of intemperate legislation. The sheer mass of 435 House members, many young and holding their first elective offices, can also suggest an atmosphere of chaos. One writer recently took some poetic license, but captured an element of the House's flavor:

> Think of the House of Representatives as a huge freshman dorm on a college campus. Everyone is adjusting to living away from home for the first time. Just like college freshmen they [fool] around all term and then pull all-nighters to get the most minimal work done. . . . [1]

House members and senators draw the same base salaries, and are theoretically equal members of Congress. In fact, seven states with small populations, like South Dakota, have only one congressional district, which means their sole "at large" member of Congress represents their entire state, just as their two senators do. But while House members often run for Senate, as I did, senators rarely run for House seats—not even in states with only one congressional district. It's considered a step down. One of my heroes actually did do that. Claude Pepper represented Florida in the Senate and was defeated in 1950 in a very ugly race. He went on to run for a House seat and won. During nearly forty years in the House, he became chairman of the Rules Committee and contributed substantially to good public policy, serving until he died in 1989.

The Senate's early gestures to show superiority over the House did not go over well. Senators suggested getting nominally higher pay and proposed a plan for delivering messages between the two chambers. The Senate secretary would deliver legislation and other documents to the House. But senators wanted at least two House members to deliver legislation to the Senate. For other paperwork, one member would suffice. The House laughed and sent its clerk.

A piece of lore recorded by an early historian, Moncure Conway, captures the relationship within the Capitol: In 1789, Thomas Jefferson returned from France after the Constitution had been adopted, and asked George Washington over breakfast why he had allowed creation of a second chamber of Congress, the Senate, beside the House of Representatives. Washington pointed to Jefferson's coffee. "Why," Washington asked, "did you pour that coffee into that saucer?"

"To cool it," Jefferson replied.

"Even so," said Washington, "we pour legislation into the senatorial saucer to cool it."

In some versions of the story, the beverage changed from coffee to tea, which led to calling the Senate "the saucer that cools the tea," for its role in tempering—and sometimes killing—fiery legislation that comes over from the House

As the nation's population continued to grow, the House's roll grew with it, beginning with 65 congressmen and reaching 435 House members in 1911. At that point, worried that House leaders wouldn't be able to manage a larger group, Congress capped the number at 435. But while the number of representatives has remained fixed for a century, the population has kept growing, now nearing an average of 700,000 souls in each congressional district. Every ten years, the districts are realigned with the census.

Meanwhile, the Great Compromise made the U.S. Senate the only legislative body in the nation that doesn't operate according to one-person, one-vote. The Senate system, by giving all states an equal voice, gives small states a big advantage. Small states get a much louder voice per capita. A majority of senators represent a tiny minority of the U.S. population. Half of all Americans live in ten states, represented by a total of twenty senators. The other half live in the forty least populous states, represented by eighty senators. In the House, by contrast, a majority of members represent the majority of the U.S. population. My home state of South Dakota exercises a voice in the Senate equal to that of California, for example, while in the House, South Dakota has only one representative while California has fifty-three.

☆ 8. DIFFERENT STROKES ☆

The sheer number of House members alone demands that the House and Senate are run in different ways. The House requires more discipline and more of a constrained environment. To oversimplify a bit, the House stresses majority rule while the Senate celebrates individual rights.

You only have to explore the role of the two Rules Committees to see the dramatic differences between the House and Senate. The House Rules Committee sets the terms for debate on every bill. How much time each side has to speak, how long the debate will last, what types of amendments are allowed, and so on. The Senate has no rules committee for that purpose. The Senate Rules Committee allocates offices and parking spaces. In the Senate, debate is generally open and limitless, with some exceptions.

Sometimes Senate leaders envy the House's tighter rules. My successor as Senate Democratic Leader, Harry Reid of Nevada, said on the Senate floor:

There are times, I can tell my colleagues without any reservation, when I wish I were the Speaker of the House. The Speaker of the House doesn't have to worry about the minority, they run over everybody. That is the way it is set up. But here, the Founding Fathers those many years ago when they came up with this unique experiment called the Congress, a bicameral legislature, those wise men set up this situation so that one house if you are in control—if one party is in control, they can do anything they want, and in the other house—the Senate—if one party is in control they can do some things they want but not everything, because the minority has tremendous power in the Senate.[1]

Senators represent broader and more diverse constituencies than House members, which generally produces less ideological divide in the Senate. But there is still a divide, which has been growing in recent years as some newly elected senators import the House's more confrontational tactics. Still, more senators are used to working in a collegial way with the other side.

The Senate is becoming more like the House in other ways, too. Increasingly, senators have been ignoring the greater national interest in pursuing their parochial state interests. And senators now often act like House members, perpetually in election cycle. In the final two years of their terms, especially, senators can spend inordinate amounts of time raising funds, away from their legislative duties.

Senators, more removed from immediate political pressures through longer terms, should focus more on the bigger, broader picture and reflect the national interest as well as their states' interests. Then-Senator John F. Kennedy wrote in *Profiles in Courage*:

For in Washington we are "United States Senators" and members of the Senate of the United States as well as senators from Massachusetts and Texas. Our oath is administered by the Vice President, not by the Governors of our respective states; and we come to Washington, to paraphrase Edmund Burke, not as hostile ambassadors or special pleaders for our state or section, in opposition to advocates and agents of other areas, but as members of the deliberative assembly of one nation with one interest.[2]

9. CHECKS AND BALANCES

An old adage holds that Congress was created by geniuses so it could be run by idiots. And the Senate has withstood more than two hundred years of mistakes and missteps—even outright attempts by so many of its members through so many years to change the framers' vision of the institution. The Senate's framework has adapted to meet modern challenges that were unimaginable when it was created nearly two and a half centuries ago. What a testament to our Founding Fathers' foresight, brilliance, and insight into the human spirit—both its dark and bright sides—that they could create such a resilient and adaptive system of government. The question now is whether it is adaptive enough. Most Americans think the federal government is now dysfunctional, unable to deal with some of our country's most pressing problems, including the budget, economy, education, and infrastructure.

The other branches—the Executive (the president) and the Judicial (the courts)—have also evolved and endured. The Constitution calls Congress the first branch of government and gives it "all legislative power." The Framers created a system of limited government, with checks and balances and separation of powers, to prevent any one branch or element from consolidating control. The president, Congress, and the courts all need the others' cooperation or consent to take action.

The Constitution did not so much divide power among the branches as it forced them to share it, each craving a larger share.[1] As future President James Madison wrote more than two hundred years ago: "Ambition must be made to counteract ambition."

The balance shifts among the branches with the players and their abilities. But presidential power has gradually grown over the centuries, while Congress has grown in size—measured by number of members and staff and Capitol Hill's expanding footprint—but has essentially kept its original authority.

Members of Congress have balked in recent decades at what they see as an increasingly "activist" federal bench willing to weigh in on—and often rule out—congressional action. The judiciary referees disputes between the legislative and executive branches, with the power to rule congressional acts and presidential actions unconstitutional and illegal. In June 2012, the Supreme Court upheld President Obama's watershed health care law, though the Court limited the law's expansion of Medicaid, the joint federal and state program for the poor and disabled. In a landmark case of judicial activism with a profound effect on the country, the Supreme Court in *Bush v. Gore* in December 2000 stopped recounts of disputed Florida ballots and essentially gave the presidency to George W. Bush in the election between Bush and then-Vice President Al Gore.

The supremacy of "Judicial Review"—giving the courts the final say—remains a pillar of our system, going back to the 1803 Supreme Court decision in *Marbury v. Madison*. Members of

Congress must consider, when crafting a given piece of legislation, how the courts might treat it.

All federal judges get lifetime appointments once nominated by the president and confirmed by the Senate, largely to shield them from politics and pressure. More than one president and senator have lamented—no longer with the power to do anything about it—that a judge's rulings were not what they had expected from the nominee they had named or approved. The line between the legislative and executive branches is not always as sharp as the lines with the judicial branch. The Constitution directs the president to give Congress information on the State of the Union and to "recommend" measures. And the vice president serves as president of the Senate.

☆ 10. SPEAKING ☆

A key difference between senators and House members is the amount of time they're permitted to speak in floor debate. Congressmen get five minutes, and senators get an unlimited amount of floor time. It's not uncommon to allocate thirty seconds to a congressman during a debate. Very rarely would you do that in the Senate, probably only at the end, facing agreed-to time limits. The rare time constraints in the Senate are in keeping with the character and the very essence of what the Senate is supposed to be.

Former Vice President Al Gore used to tell a story about his early career in Washington. He served in the House for a number of years, then came to the Senate, and others gathered around for his maiden speech. Because Gore was so instinctively trained to speak for five minutes, he gave his five-minute speech. But there was a sense of expectation in the Senate, and some of his new colleagues asked him why he had spoken such a short amount of time. That was all the notes he had, however, so Gore just repeated that same speech in different forms three or four more times, finishing out his five-minute speech over the course of a half hour. The others were satisfied.

It's also said that the Senate is the only place in the country where somebody stands up to speak, nobody listens, and then everybody disagrees. There's a lot of truth to that. People do speak, and it appears that nobody's listening. And certainly there's a lot of disagreement.

As Senate Majority Leader Robert Taft said in 1939:

> I came from a state legislature, where people made speeches to other people to persuade them that they ought to vote for or against a bill; but speeches in the Senate are apparently made to the people back home, or to the press gallery. I know they are not real speeches, because no other Senator stays to listen to them.

And that was in the days before the Senate was televised and members began speaking to the cameras.

My transition from the House to the Senate was largely a matter of adjusting to more speaking, in the spirit of Al Gore's anecdote, and extemporaneous speaking, especially as Leader.

For most people in politics, if they're not comfortable speaking and expressing themselves on their feet when they get to the floor of a legislature, over time they learn to be more comfortable. But it's also a matter of style. Some senators prefer to be very tightly scripted, and will only read what they have in front of them. Their talking points produced by their staff may begin, "Good morning, I'm Senator X." Very rarely will they speak extemporaneously, or off the cuff.

Then there are other senators who will never use a text. In the Senate, especially, you have the luxury to place a speech in the *Congressional Record*, the daily transcript of House and Senate action, as if it had been given—even if you never actually spoke a word of it. And there's no way to tell by looking at the *Record* what was spoken live and what was inserted—to figure that out, you'd have to sift through the video archives.

I generally found myself in the middle, between scripted and extemporaneous. I liked to scribble some handwritten notes and speak from those. My approach had a lot to do with my comfort level with the given subject matter. A Leader is required to talk about more than just issues; you talk about the schedule. And you're often required to deal with subjects that are not part of your own issue base. So the less confident you were about an issue, the more text-reliant you would often be.

Whatever is said—or not said—on the Senate floor is open to the public. The Constitution doesn't require Congress to hold open sessions, only to publish a journal of its proceedings "from time to time." But senators want their constituents to see them at work. Congress does more business in public view than either of the other branches, and also publishes most of it in hearing transcripts, reports, and other documents. And the *Congressional Record* carries everything that senators said on the floor—and some things they didn't say.

II. THE VP: PRESIDENT OF THE SENATE

☆ ☆

The Constitution names the vice president of the United States as president of the Senate. But while the vice president may preside over sessions of the Senate, he or she casts votes only to break ties.

Vice presidents learned early—and sometimes painfully—of the limits of their power over the Senate. Our nation's first vice president, John Adams, annoyed senators with what some considered patronizing lectures. At the outset of the Washington administration, Adams mused publicly about how to address the new president and vice president, since the VP would also serve as president of the Senate. When Adams suggested "His Majesty" as a possibility, some senators began calling Adams—who was short and squat—"His Rotundity." A friend warned Adams that "he who mingles in debate subjects himself to frequent retorts from his opposers, places himself on the same ground with his inferiors in rank, appears too much like the leader of a party, and renders it more difficult for him to support the dignity of the chair and to preserve order and regularity in debate." Adams told his friend, "I have no desire ever to open my mouth again upon any question." And, for the rest of his term as vice president, he rarely did.

Ever since, vice presidents have taken Adams's approach in the Senate. For nearly two hundred years, through then-Vice President Nixon's tenure under President Eisenhower, presiding over the Senate was the VP's main function. The vice president operated from an office in the Capitol and rarely attended cabinet meetings or other executive activities.

Lyndon Johnson won elections in November 1960 for both vice president and senator, after having Texas law changed to allow him to run for both offices. Johnson devised a plan to effectively keep his Majority Leader post, even as he resigned from the Senate, by serving as Chairman of the Senate's Democratic Caucus, a job that routinely went to the Majority Leader. Johnson figured that the vice president already presided over the Senate and broke tie votes, so this would be another similar duty. Johnson privately ran his plan by a few key senators. They didn't want to say no to him, leaving Johnson believing that he had persuaded them to go along. He also wanted to keep the Capitol office that he had used as Majority Leader, which he called the "Taj Mahal" and is now called the LBJ Room. Johnson convinced incoming Majority Leader Mike Mansfield to nominate him as caucus chairman, on the understanding that the title would be merely honorary. But Johnson planned to attend and preside over Democratic caucus meetings. When Mansfield made the nomination at a fateful caucus meeting, senators revolted, saying Johnson would shatter the separation of powers among the branches and make the Senate "look ridiculous." Shocked, Johnson turned ashen. Mansfield threatened to step down if his colleagues rejected his motion, so Democratic senators gave Johnson the title. But LBJ got the message, and did not attend a caucus for nearly two years, until

January 1963. By then, Robert Caro wrote, "his attendance was no longer a threat to anyone, since by that time Washington understood that he had lost all his power, so completely that he had become almost a figure of ridicule in the capital."[1]

LBJ fundamentally changed the vice presidency by moving his main office to the White House from the Capitol and focusing on executive business, presiding over the Senate only at key times that might demand his vote or ruling. Ever since, vice presidents have followed Johnson's model.

Walter Mondale, another senator turned vice president, summarized: "For most of our history, since the Vice Presidents were in both branches, they have been treated as if they were in neither."[2]

President George H. W. Bush recalled that, as vice president, he cast seven tie-breaking Senate votes—three of them on the dicey matter of nerve gas.

A myth arose from one of those votes that my mother bawled me out. Well, she didn't quite do that. She did give advice, however. After attending my first State of the Union speech as Vice President, for example, Mother called to say she had noticed that I was talking to [House Speaker] Tip O'Neill while President Reagan was addressing the country. "He started it," was all I could think to say.

"Another thing," she continued. "You should try smiling more."

"But Mum, the President was talking about nuclear annihilation."[3]

In the vice president's absence, under the Constitution, the Senate's "President pro tempore" presides. The title is Latin for "for the time being," and is often shortened to President pro tem.

Elected by the Senate, the President pro tempore is customarily the majority party's most senior member, sometimes past ninety years old. The President pro tem is third in line to succeed the president of the United States, after the vice president and Speaker of the House.

The job of President pro tempore evolved from an ad hoc position for short periods to an indefinite term. At first, when vice presidents regularly presided over the Senate, senators named a president pro tempore only for stints when a vice president was away, selecting "on the basis of their personal characteristics, popularity, and reliability," as Senator Robert Byrd put it. Since 1890, Presidents pro tem have served until a new one was elected— which generally meant until they retired, died, or their party lost the majority.

But, tuning into C-SPAN, you'll seldom see the stately senior President pro tem wielding the gavel. He or she generally delegates that job, on a rotating basis, to the majority party's junior members. It's a right of passage for new senators, and a chance to learn the Senate rules in combat situations.

The Senate hasn't always chosen its Presidents pro tem smoothly. In 1911, the Senate deadlocked for three months between a Democratic member who had unanimous Democratic support and a Republican member whose party held the majority, because eight Republican insurgents voted for other candidates. Eventually, senators compromised on a rotating schedule of Presidents pro tempore, including the Democrat.

12. THE WORKERS AND THE WORKLOAD

☆ ☆

Senators' jobs primarily involve advancing legislation, performing executive oversight, considering nominations, and providing services to their constituents. The work is non-stop and the days are long, filled with meetings, hearings, media interviews, speeches, events, and phone calls, all punctuated by votes.

The pace has been this way for decades, worsened, arguably, by the longer sessions, shorter work weeks, 24/7 news cycle, the Internet, BlackBerrys, and SmartPhones.

Donald Matthews wrote in his 1960 classic, *U.S. Senators and Their World*, which largely remains timeless:

> "But it's not the hard work or the long hours that wear you down," one Senator explained, "it's the *uncertainty*. You never know when there will be a crisis, a roll call, when the session will run into the evening, or if there will be a Friday or Saturday session. You don't even know when Congress will adjourn."[1]

Senators—and their staffs—yearn for a session's adjournment like students awaiting summer vacation. As another veteran Senate watcher wrote:

Adjournment is the spring unwound, the last frantic push to get home before the opposition back in the states can gain ground. With few exceptions, Capitol Hill succumbs to adjournment fever, a virulent disease that overpowers legislators and propels them madly to the end. Carefully studied legislation is jettisoned; hastily-put-together compromises are accepted. . . . Staff members and legislators rush around at a feverish pace to arrange the necessary conferences. Out of this chaos comes the realization that many bills must be abandoned."[2]

A U.S. Senate seat offers power, prestige, and sometimes fame, and an extraordinary opportunity to render public service, Matthews concluded. "Yet the price of power is high. Few Americans could live with the job's tensions, moral dilemmas, intrigue and insecurity. . . . An almost superhuman vitality is needed to cope with the job's work load. Certainly, few could be attracted to the job by the pay."[3]

The Senate is called both the world's greatest deliberative body and the most exclusive club. Senators can develop severe cases of "Potomac Fever," an immersion in the Capitol culture including a sense that the world revolves around Washington's events—and, to an extent, around *them*. Senate Republican Leader Hugh Scott said, "Every Senator dances on his own center stage."[4]

An old quip holds that every senator looks in the mirror and sees a future president. President Woodrow Wilson offered his own dig: "Every man who takes office in Washington either grows or swells." Another observer wrote:

The senatorial system tends to sow arrogance in its members, what Senator John F. Kennedy of Massachusetts once called, quoting Hamlet, "the insolence of office." Rare indeed is the politician who does not provide a fertile field for haughtiness with its own inherently egocentric view of life.[5]

Many senators are humble, decent, and courteous to their staffs, colleagues, and constituents alike, and even to their opponents. But the archetype is more blustery. As Republican Leader Taft said in 1939:

> Although there are ninety-six Senators, the employees around the Senate manage to say, "Yes, Senator" and "No, Senator" as if each Senator were the father of his country. And so it isn't hard for any senator to come to believe that most fatal of all illusions, that the country or his party hangs upon his words and can't get on without him.

Senators disproportionately come from the ranks of lawyers and business executives, with a share of professors and publishers, and an occasional doctor and homemaker. They have generally distinguished themselves in previous public office or in other fields.

Law, especially, makes a natural political route, as Matthews noted. Many elective offices, including judge and prosecutor posts, are open only to lawyers. Lawyers' schedules allow time for politicking, and a lawyer's skills in debate, negotiating, and formulating and arguing a case on a client's behalf are all easily transferable to the Senate.

Still, while senators and representatives make the nation's laws, there's no requirement to hold a law degree in order to serve in Congress. Roughly half of the senators are lawyers. I was among the other half, and while I consider a legal education valuable, it's not essential. Senator Dianne Feinstein of California has served with distinction for years on the Judiciary Committee, and she does not have a law degree. Other attributes—including experience, judgment, savvy, tenacity, and the ability to build relationships and coalitions—are at least as important as a J.D. Many senators have held previous elected office. I, for instance, served in the House. Others, have served in some state elected capacity. I found that the group that had the hardest time adjusting to Senate life was former governors, perhaps because as chief executives they had so much authority and autonomy. They didn't have to get fifty-nine other people to agree with them to do something. They also had far more staff.

Many senators, including those who go on to even higher office, cite their time in the Senate as the happiest of their careers. Truman described his decade in the Senate as "filled with hard work but which were also to be the happiest ten years of my life."[6]

Vice President Mondale said:

My Senate years were the happiest of my public career. I found my sweet spot here. I loved working with friends and colleagues, and I loved learning new things. I loved watching my colleagues do their stuff. . . . Eighteen hours a day, every day, it was like mainlining human nature.[7]

☆ 13. SENATE STAFF ☆

Watch a Senate hearing, and you'll see a row of senators behind a long dais, constantly swiveling their chairs to huddle with aides and to sign and swap papers. Look at a newspaper photo of a senator striding down a corridor, and you'll usually see aides flanking the lawmaker, matching their boss's stride. You won't see the aides' names on a C-SPAN crawler or in the photo caption, but the senators couldn't do their jobs without their staff. I was extraordinarily fortunate to have such a good, hardworking, and dedicated staff, beginning with two chiefs of staff, Pete Stavrianos and Pete Rouse. I have often been told that I had the best staff of any office on the Hill.

Six thousand staffers support our one hundred senators. They do the legwork and groundwork, so that senators can go into a hearing or debate prepared, armed with facts and background on the issues, and—for those senators who prefer to read from notes—a script on what to say.

The average staffer is young, many in their early or mid-twenties and fresh out of college or law school. College students who intern on Capitol Hill often return after graduation as permanent staff. Congressional fellows, borrowed from various organizations or agencies, and pages also often come back. In recent decades, staff jobs have served increasingly as springboards to Senate seats.

I began in Washington as a Senate staffer. Over mild objections from my parents, I had majored in political science, in part because I wanted to make politics my career. After college, I was serving in the Air Force and stationed near Omaha. Nebraska was an important primary state in the 1972 presidential race, so after hours, I volunteered on George McGovern's campaign. Congressman Jim Abourezk, who was campaigning for McGovern there, asked if I wanted to join him on his Senate campaign. As I was leaving the Air Force, I was very happy to accept his offer. Abourezk won and asked me to come to D.C. as a legislative aide.

A number of my Senate interns and junior staff have also gone on to important careers in the Senate and beyond, with several taking high-level positions in the Obama administration, including the White House Counsel to the president, Pete Rouse.

One dedicated and diligent intern, Grant Leslie, in 2001 opened a seemingly innocuous white envelope addressed to my office, bearing a return address from "4th Grade, Greendale School, Franklin Park, NJ." Anthrax spores poured out, unleashing the biggest bioterrorist attack in U.S. history. Grant recovered, graduated from college, and returned to join my permanent staff.

A politically minded young person can rise to a position of responsibility as a Hill staffer faster than almost anywhere else. But just as for their bosses, the pace and the work are brutal and the pay is generally low. Some Senate staffers burn out or move on after a few years, having gained vital experience and insight on how government works. For those who stay on the Hill, some move from "personal staff," based in a senator's office, to a "professional" committee staff, joining a team of issue experts, typically through appointment from a senator to a committee on which he serves. The committee staffer will cover meetings for senators, advise them on issues and votes and negotiate legislation. Staffers who wield such authority are often called "unelected lawmakers" and "virtual senators."[1] Most committee staff positions, though, are strictly legislative and somewhat removed from the day-to-day bustle of Senate activity. Committee staff have little constituent interaction, little routine connection with senators or work diversity. In no way is this meant to minimize their role. They are oftentimes more senior and more issue driven than "Senator-driven." But many staff prefer a personal office role than one on a committee.

In the Senate, you may also notice youths hustling around wearing navy suits, white shirts and name plates. They're pages, high school juniors at least sixteen years old playing an important role in the Senate and enjoying a rare chance to immerse themselves in Congress and in Washington. Daniel Webster selected the first pages in the early nineteenth century, and senators still appoint and sponsor pages. The second page ever to serve, Isaac Bassett, kept an amazing journal, in which he vividly described Webster yelling at him for making a mistake involving his carriage and how his hair began turning white shortly thereafter. Bassett went on to become assistant doorkeeper, ultimately serving sixty-four years in the Senate.

Page life is not easy. On a typical day, pages are in school by 6:15 a.m. After several hours, they report to the Capitol to prepare the Senate chamber for the day's session. Throughout the day, they are called upon to perform a wide array of tasks—from obtaining copies of documents and reports for senators to use during debate, to running errands between the Capitol and the Senate office buildings, to lending a hand at our weekly conference luncheons.

Once senators finish their business for the day—no matter what time—the pages return to the dorm and prepare for the next day's classes and Senate session and, one hopes, to get some much-needed sleep.

The page program is a treasure. Pages are not only spectators to the democratic experiment, but real participants. Each becomes all the more adept at all of their responsibilities as the session unfolds and they become students of government in a unique and special way. At graduations for our pages, I often urged them to consider coming back, not only as members of the staff, but perhaps one day as elected members themselves. I was confident that, at some point, some of them would.

David Pryor, a congressman and senator from Arkansas, began his public service as a House page during the summer of 1951, before his senior year at high school in Camden, Arkansas. That summer, young David wedged a dime in a crevice behind a pillar in the Capitol basement. He hoped to return one day as a member and find it. In 1967, when newly elected Congressman Pryor returned to Washington, he did find the dime—and left it there. Construction has since covered the area.[2] Pryor's story is a testament to the dreams, aspirations, and remarkable persistence that our pages often have—and to the page program itself. You get inspired.

The House, as a cost-cutting measure, eliminated its page program in August 2011, which I found very disappointing. The relatively minimal cost made the page program one of best investments Congress makes, and we have to encourage young people to get involved politically and in public service. I'm very pleased that the Senate has chosen to keep its page program, and I hope that the House will bring theirs back

14. CONSTITUENT SERVICE

☆ ☆

Senators generally make weekly trips home, often rushing to the airport or the train station Thursday or Friday when the Senate recesses, and returning Monday or Tuesday when the Senate reconvenes. They also spend the bulk of most recesses, which some senators call "work periods," in their states. Senators might meet with constituents at their state offices or at public forums, hold press events to announce funding for a bridge or highway or levee, tour a promising new manufacturing plant, speak at service club lunches, ride in parades, or participate in a host of other local events.

I held "open door" meetings, where I invited the public to come to a local café. I used the term since we knocked on forty thousand doors in my first campaign. At one open-door meeting in a café-bar in a very small town, a man who seemed to have been drinking all day interrupted me to ask, "Daschle, what is the difference between a Republican and a Democrat?"

"When you sober up, I will tell you," I replied. He then quipped, "When I am sober, I don't give a damn!"

I also used to get in my car by myself for a week or so at a time and just drive to the distant corners of my state with no staff or schedule. I would just show up. I interviewed small business owners, spoke impromptu to school assemblies, and even knocked on doors. I enjoyed it immensely.

Largely, senators are informing and accounting to their constituents—their bosses, who elected them and who can fire them next time the senator's job goes on the ballot. But the contact is hardly one way. The First Amendment to the Constitution gives Americans the right to petition their government, and they do. Letters, phone calls, and e-mails pour into Senate offices on the gamut of issues. Mostly, people want the senator to vote a certain way on a bill; or they want help cutting through the red tape of federal bureaucracy, such as straightening out a snag with Social Security or veterans payments, expediting a passport, or nominating a son or daughter for admission to a military service academy.

E-mail, which began in the 1990s, now accounts for 80 percent of all congressional correspondence. The use of e-mail accelerated after the package of weapons-grade anthrax arrived at my Hart Building office in October 2001, eventually forcing the months-long closure and sterilization of the entire structure.

But there's an old adage that "good government is good politics," and senators must constantly demonstrate to their bosses back home what they're doing to move the country forward and to make sure their state "gets its fair share" of federal resources. Senators must compete for limited federal funds to "bring home the bacon" for what they each consider important local projects, but which others may call "pork." New York Senator Alfonse D'Amato focused so heavily on delivering federal funds for his state that he was known as "Senator Pothole."

Still, one concern is that members are now spending too much time in their states and districts and not enough time in Washington. Many so-called "legislative days" are really only pro forma legislative sessions. Many problems come from too much time away, including lack of time and ability to do serious work, little interaction among members, therefore less bonding and relationship-building, and no chance to build momentum for difficult legislative projects.

Some years ago, when senators had greater opportunity to provide earmarks, directing funds toward particular projects or programs in their states, some abuses soiled a process that was already under scrutiny. Alaska's "Bridge to Nowhere" drew enormous ridicule. The project got a $223 million earmark in 2005 to link Ketchikan, population nine thousand, to Gravina Island, which had only a few dozen residents. Senator William Proxmire used to present "Golden Fleece Awards" to U.S. officials who, by his reckoning, had wasted taxpayers' money. In the same spirit, the watchdog group Citizens Against Government Waste presents a "Porker of the Year Award."

At this writing, earmarking has been banned, at least temporarily, under a voluntary moratorium. I actually support earmarks, so long as the practice is not abused and is completely transparent. In my opinion, helping to decide the prioritization of federal investments in states should be the responsibility of elected officials, not of unelected and unknown decision makers in the executive branch, though not everyone would agree on that.

The opportunity to provide constituent service, along with other opportunities of incumbency (holding office) offer enormous advantages when it comes time to run for reelection. But they're not insurmountable. I beat an incumbent senator in 1986 to win my seat. I eventually lost my seat in 2004 to a challenger. I was the Democratic Leader at the time, so that race took on a national scale and saw an unprecedented barrage by the other party.

The system has taken steps to level the playing field. Letters and newsletters back home—sent at taxpayers' expense, though now delivered online more than through the mail—offer a good way to let constituents know what the senator has been doing— for the country and for them. But those mass mailings are now prohibited for senators within several months of their elections, as are postings on their official Web sites.

15. SENATE LEADERSHIP

The Framers didn't mention Senate Majority and Minority Leaders in the Constitution because American political parties didn't exist when they wrote it. Until the early twentieth century, the President pro tempore and chairmen of major committees largely led the Senate. The Majority and Minority Leaders formally came into being in 1913, when President Wilson convinced Senate Democrats to appoint a floor leader to manage his legislative agenda. Whips also came into being in 1913. The term "whip" does not come from an enforcer who lashes senators into compliance, as some might think. Rather, "whip" comes from the fox-hunting term "whipper-in," for the team member responsible for keeping the dogs from straying during a chase. Both parties in the Senate elect whips. The Senate Democratic caucus, irked by chronically poor attendance at its caucus meetings, adopted the idea from both parties in the House. Senate Republicans followed two years later. By 1937, the Senate floor had taken the layout we see today, with the Majority and Minority Leaders' desks front and center, their deputies—the party whips—beside them. But the Majority Leader's job didn't take on its modern power until Lyndon Johnson held the position from 1955 to 1961.

I began my leadership career, when I was a young new congressman, by winning election as a regional whip in the House. A mentor, Congressman Mo Udall of Arizona, suggested that I run for the job, partly to help build relationships with colleagues. The regional whips served as contacts for head counts on particular votes and relayed messages between the leadership and members. I was whip for the Rocky Mountain region.

When I moved from the House to the Senate in 1987, Democratic Leader George Mitchell also became a mentor and put me on the Senate leadership ladder. I was the first cochair of the Senate Democratic Policy Committee. The Leader had always had the prerogative to hold that job exclusively, but Mitchell offered me a spot as cochair. Republicans arrange their party leadership organization differently from the Democrats, but the policy chair, in both caucuses, has significant responsibility. The jobs are important in the leadership structure, and fulfilling. In the Democratic Policy Committee post, you have four main responsibilities:

First, and most basic, you need to inform your members about the legislative agenda. As part of that role, the policy committee chair organized retreats for the caucus. We used to hold a daylong retreat and then a two-day retreat each year. The retreats have since become more sporadic, but they're still held.

Second, the Policy Committee keeps the historical records on members' votes and other legislative activities.

Third, the policy chair handles issue-related functions within the caucus. As an example, I originated the practice of bringing in historians and other experts to talk about particular issues at our Thursday caucus lunch meetings. A lot of members who didn't serve on committees that oversaw particular issues of interest to them weren't hearing about developments on those issues, and I wanted to give them opportunities to do so. The lunches were all done very informally, off the record, and involved only members of the Senate.

Finally, the policy committee chair directs what we commonly call special projects. One of my first assignments when I became policy chair was to talk to all caucus members, and in particular the committee chairs, about health reform, to get a consensus about what we should do on the issue. That's really how I got as interested in health policy as I did.

In early 1994, Senator Mitchell announced his retirement, and I decided to run for his job. My move raised a lot of eyebrows, both in the cloakroom and in the press gallery. I had served only eight years in the Senate. Only one senator had risen to Majority Leader in less time—LBJ, elected Leader in 1954, after just six years. Further, some questioned whether I was tough enough. I'd never chaired a committee, and so had never led my team in closed-door committee-room battles. More than one reporter dismissed me as a "back-bencher." Another called me a "park ranger in a dark suit." Some senior caucus colleagues found me too low-key, understated, and soft-spoken to lead the coming fights against the Republican majority.

I wasn't surprised by any of the doubts about me. I think I've benefited my whole life from low expectations and from being underestimated. When I announced my candidacy for the House back in 1978, some people laughed. As I was campaigning door-to-door in South Dakota, one person mistook me for the paperboy. I had drawn the same type of reaction when I first ran for the Senate. But I had worked hard through the policy committee post to build strong individual relationships.

The vote for Majority Leader came down to a 23–23 tie with Chris Dodd of Connecticut, a close friend. I won—by a margin of one vote—on a proxy from Ben Nighthorse Campbell. I had asked Campbell for the proxy, not even knowing if it would be honored, when he told me he wouldn't be in town for the vote. The margin fed my nickname "Landslide Daschle," first earned through some tight congressional elections. Shortly after that election, Ben switched from Democrat to Republican. That triggered a good natured-call from Chris Dodd suggesting a recount.

In Senate leadership on the Democratic side, several chairs play significant roles, in addition to the policy chair: The Democratic Senate Campaign Committee (DSCC) chair is probably the hardest job to fill because it involves so much work, travel, and pressure to raise funds. Often, understandings are made that if a senator takes that role, he or she will get further opportunities within the caucus or within the Senate, such as committee assignments. It's no coincidence that a large number of the DSCC chairs also serve on the most sought-after committee, Finance.

In the 1990s, I created the Democratic Technology and Communications Committee (DTCC) and named Jay Rockefeller as its first chair, since he was likely to become chair of the Commerce Committee. The DTCC's purpose, primarily, was to integrate technological innovation with the broad array of caucus activities. People were just starting to understand what computers were all about, just starting to routinely tap satellite video communication to their states. I was concerned that we needed a new technological paradigm. We actually built a studio with state-of-the-art equipment. Now, everybody's got BlackBerrys and iPhones, but the DTCC was largely in charge of coordinating that.

When I began as Leader, I also built up the Steering Committee, whose only job had been making committee membership decisions. I added "Coordination" to the name, since I wanted more coordination among Senate Democrats and community leaders across the nation. But we then had two DSCCs, the Democratic Senate Campaign Committee and the Democratic Steering and Coordination Committee. So we changed the name to the Democratic Steering and Outreach Committee, so that we could distinguish one from the other. We hadn't been doing enough to reach out to constituency groups and to other groups beyond our base. So my thought was, let's bring in different groups that have concerns about issues they think we should know about, and talk about ways we might work more closely together.

16. LOADING FROGS INTO A WHEELBARROW

The Senate, to an extent, is a preserve of one hundred independent contractors. And they are all very ambitious, many of them convinced they should be president of the United States, or at least that they could do the job as well as whoever is occupying the White House at the time. The Democratic caucus, especially, values and encourages diversity and independent voices. It's not easy captaining that kind of team. An analogy around Capitol Hill holds that leading the Senate is like herding cats. I often likened the job to loading frogs into a wheelbarrow.

The job has arguably grown tougher in recent years, with the rising partisan strife. Majority Leader Baker said while I was Democratic Leader, "I herded cats. Trent Lott and Tom Daschle have to tame tigers."[1]

One of the biggest misperceptions of a Majority Leader is that he has all these powerful tools to craft the Senate agenda and get his way. But a Majority Leader can't dictate, either to individual senators or to committees. LBJ, as Majority Leader, used to say that the only power he had was the power of persuasion.

My predecessor, George Mitchell, agreed. "What influence I have is based upon . . . respect and reasoned persuasion and some sensitivity to the political and other concerns of individual Senators," he said. "I don't have a large bag of goodies to hand out to Senators nor do I have any mechanism for disciplining Senators."[2]

People might be surprised to know that a Majority Leader really has only three tools. In order of importance, they are:

1. The right of recognition—A Majority Leader is always recognized first, if he seeks to speak on the floor. If you control the floor, you control what comes afterward.

2. The art of persuasion—A Leader must employ a whole spectrum of persuasive options, from plain reason to politics, emotion, personal relationships, threats, to even using surrogates—that is, sending other senators to plead your cause with particular colleagues, often without explicitly noting that they're acting on your behalf. Leaders use all of those tools, and use them frequently.

3. Committee assignments—The Majority Leader is the ultimate decision maker on assignments, at least technically; he can put a senator on a committee and, though it's rarely done, he can yank somebody off a committee. However, now a Leader needs approval from the Steering and Outreach Committee and the caucus to change committee membership. Still, that realization is pretty potent when it comes to persuasion.

The Leader also controls the schedule. That, too, can be a critical tool, such as by threatening to keep senators in session on weekends or during recesses. A Leader also has access to the national media, which provides an opportunity to frame the issues. Leaders regularly appear on the Sunday-morning network public affairs shows such as *Meet the Press, This Week,* and *Face the Nation,* and get quoted in national newspapers.

How does a Leader learn how to persuade other senators? By the time you become Leader, you've been on the receiving end of a lot of that persuasive effort yourself, so you know how it works. You've watched others who were good at it work their skills in other settings. In my case, some of the people with whom I worked were particularly persuasive. House Speaker Tip O'Neill was extraordinary. Speaker Jim Wright and House Ways and Means Chairman Dan Rostenkowski (D-Ill.) were both very persuasive. On the Senate side, George Mitchell and Robert Byrd were pros.

Also, as Leader, your position has an aura, which creates more of a persuasive persona. If you're the Leader or the Speaker, there's a respect for the office and for the position that gives you—if used appropriately—a very effective tool in getting your caucus to do what needs to be done.

One of the most persuasive tools, in my experience as Democratic Leader, is the weekly Democratic caucus-wide lunch meeting from 1 to 2 p.m. on Tuesdays. It's the single most important hour of the whole week, in many respects. Lunch begins at 12:30 p.m. and the meeting actually starts at 1 o'clock and usually goes to about 2:15, though it's supposed to end at 2 o'clock. That gives you roughly an hour or an hour and a quarter, and you first spend a lot of time with your staff preparing for the meeting. You nail down what needs to be covered and how to talk about it, even to the point that you orchestrate strategically calling upon members who can augment your arguments. I'd call on respected leaders within the caucus, more senior members who chaired an important committee and could often supplement or bolster my arguments. And you make your best case. I often used PowerPoints. PowerPoints may have lost some of their traction over the years, but there's something about a visual that can make a real difference.

I regret that we didn't host more bipartisan caucus meetings. Those we did hold often dealt with a crisis, such as impeachment, and the September 11 and anthrax attacks. More bipartisan experiences might have increased cooperation and reduced polarization in later years.

While there's an element of speaking softly and carrying a big stick, to borrow from Teddy Roosevelt, a Leader often delivers his messages frankly and explicitly. A Majority Leader might say to a senator in his caucus, "I'm never going to ask you to do something that you can't support in your conscience. But there are going to be some key votes where unless it violates your conscience, we must have a clear understanding that I'm going to have your vote."

A Leader might deliver that kind of message in appointing a senator to a sought-after committee like Finance, when the Leader knew that key votes were going to come up on tax or health or trade policy, and that the particular senator's political disposition might make him unwilling to help the team. So you call attention to the fact that he has not always voted the way you would have liked on a particular issue. You say that's going to become even more of a challenge if he ascends to the Finance Committee, because those votes happen not only on the floor, but in the committee itself. Most of the time, the votes in these committees are vital, because with such close margins between the parties, you can't afford to lose a single aye or nay, or you lose the whole vote.

There was always a handshake. There was never anything in writing. Those arrangements were understood, though they were not always remembered.

As Matthews wrote in 1960, and which still applies today:

"Most of the time," one senator explained, "the leader is cast in the position of someone trying to help you with your problems." . . . Does he need to be out of town when an important roll call vote is likely to be taken? Does he desire a seat on the Foreign Relations Committee? Wish to make a four-hour speech next Thursday? . . . As a result, the leader is in an excellent position to know every member's problems, ambitions and idiosyncrasies. If the leader makes a firm commitment to be of aid, a senator can count on his battling to keep his word—and reminding the senator of the favor if it should ever be necessary to do so![3]

I used to tell a story about a young congressman from Boston who was under a lot of pressure from Tip O'Neill to vote for something that the Speaker really wanted. The congressman said, "Mr. Speaker, this project you want just doesn't make sense. I can't support it." O'Neill replied, "Well, if it made sense, I wouldn't need your vote."

Serving as Senate Leader was an immensely rich experience. It's a combination of sporting event and political event and oftentimes a rich, historical drama that beats anything on television.

I served two tours each as Majority Leader and Minority Leader, and it's far better to hold the majority. Control of the Senate shifts periodically with elections, but one party can maintain control of the chamber for decades.

The majority, through its Leader, controls the Senate floor agenda, deciding which bills come up for votes and when. The majority names committee chairmen, who decide when to hold hearings and what legislation to send to the floor for debate. The majority also controls most of the money.

But the minority is not without tools, I found. Its ultimate weapon is the filibuster. We'll get to the details of filibusters in Part III. But for now, think of a filibuster as a tactic opponents can use to block any nomination or piece of legislation that comes to the floor, if they can muster forty votes.

In 1996, we Democrats held a filibuster through a couple of rounds of votes on a key bill in the Republicans' "Contract with America." Bob Dole, then Majority Leader, expressed frustration and exasperation that he couldn't move the legislation forward. In a brash moment, which I might have handled more diplomatically, I said, "Welcome to the Senate, Senator Dole."

The minority has much more muscle in the Senate than in the House, which goes to the heart of the difference between the House as a collective institution of majority rule and the Senate as an institution of individuals. When the majority and minority butt heads in the Senate, they often engage in a ritual in which the majority cites an electoral mandate to pass its agenda, and the minority says, "We're elected by our constituents, too, and we're going to do everything we can to stop you, don't run over us the way the majority does in the House—we can at least amend bills, if we can't pass them."

Occasionally, one party enjoys a wide, "filibuster-proof" majority in the Senate. Majority Leader Mike Mansfield commanded a 65–35 ratio in the early 1960s, and passed sweeping legislation. Some years ago, Mansfield turned to me during a speech and said, "With those numbers, anything should be possible under the lash of disciplined leadership. Think of it, Senator Daschle."[1]

But the margin between majority and minority is more often close, as it was throughout my time in the Senate. At the extreme, the 2000 election left the Senate equally divided, bringing a period of "power sharing."

Republican Leader Trent Lott had been Senate Majority Leader before that November 2000 election. When I first reached Lott after the Senate officially became fifty-fifty for the first time in history, he could hardly finish a sentence. He was in shock. His world had just been turned upside down. At first, Senate Republicans couldn't even bring themselves to utter the phrase "power sharing." "It's difficult," Senate Republican Whip Don

Nickles told a reporter, "for me to see how two people can drive a car at the same time."[2]

I've felt Trent Lott's pain; I've also gone from Majority Leader to Minority Leader. It's hard to adjust, like getting a terminal diagnosis and going through the Kübler-Ross model of the five phases of grief: denial, anger, bargaining, depression, and acceptance.

The Senate's 20 committees, 68 subcommittees, and 4 joint committees collectively handle all the issues the Senate covers. Most committees are further divided into subcommittees, to focus on particular issue areas, such as the Judiciary Subcommittee on Crime and Terrorism or the Appropriations Subcommittee on Defense.

It's said that committees are where the *real* work of the Senate is done. Nearly all legislation is referred to a committee, and sometimes to more than one. "Writing legislation on the floor"—sending matters directly for full Senate debate—doesn't allow committee experts to shape the bill first, and is discouraged.

The parties control seats on committees roughly proportional to their share of seats in the full Senate. Each senator serves on up to a dozen committees and subcommittees. Generally, every majority-party senator chairs a committee or subcommittee, and most freshmen either chair or serve as ranking minority member of a subcommittee.

Committee work is where senators establish expertise and

reputations, and make their imprint on American law and policy. A senator's committee assignments will determine much of his or her career, similar to choosing a major in college. Through committee work, senators dive into particular issues and make these issues their own, develop expert voices in subject areas, and build networks, including fund-raising networks.

The Senate must handle the same sweeping workload as the House, but with a membership less than a quarter the size. Plus, senators must also grasp the issues as they affect entire states and the nation. Together, those dynamics force senators to become generalists, even while specializing in committee issues. By contrast, House members may serve on only one major committee, and specialize early and narrowly. Two or more of a senator's committees will often meet at the same time, forcing him or her to choose among them or to bounce among hearings.

Senators seek seats on particular committees for a chance to handle issues important to them or to their constituents. I served on the Agriculture Committee, for example, largely because corn, soybeans, wheat, livestock, and other farming interests were so vital to South Dakota. Apart from any state connection, though, some committees are considered more desirable than others, thereby creating a caste system. Senators generally favor Appropriations, Finance, Judiciary, Foreign Relations, and Armed Services over Rules and Administration or Veterans Affairs, for example. The more elite committees, generally filled by the most prominent senators, offer better perches for influencing policy, gaining prominence, raising campaign funds, and staging bids for national office.

Members used to be very limited in the number of committees on which they served, for a number of reasons: It's important to keep committees small and manageable, it's easier to get a quorum with fewer members, and it's also more likely that a senator will become more expert in the given committee's issues. Now, however, it's not uncommon for a senator to sit on six committees. Each committee has a fund-raising constituency. That, in part, is what motivates senators to join. It also affords them more legislative roles. Unfortunately, absenteeism is a huge problem as a result.

Once elected, a senator's first big task is landing committee assignments. At the beginning of a Congress, each party's Steering Committee assigns new members to committees and shifts senior members to more desirable committees where vacancies have opened.

Subcommittee assignments are also key. On some committees, such as Appropriations, subcommittees do the majority of the work on legislation, especially much of the initial work. Like college admissions officers, they cull promising bills from the mass of introductions. They gather information, hold hearings, and report bills to "full committee" for further action. Most bills die in subcommittee or committee. Woodrow Wilson called committees "dim dungeons of silence."

Committees are generally less polarized than the larger Senate, their members' policy stances closer, for a variety of reasons. Over years of working together on a committee, members form friendships and understandings, even across the aisle. And committee members come to sympathize at least a bit with the agencies they oversee, from hearing those agencies' continual requests and appeals.[1] Still, some committees, notably Judiciary, are more polarized. Battles over judicial nominations often highlight the gap between the parties' orthodox views.

19. COMMITTEE CHAIRS

☆   ☆

The Senate began without permanent committees. Today's structure of twenty permanent committees grew gradually over the decades and centuries, spurred by war-driven emergencies. In the eighteenth century, several temporary "select" committees reviewed all legislation. The War of 1812 created crises that demanded prompt, expert action, and the Senate created more ad hoc committees to tackle situations as they arose. In 1816, the Senate formally converted eleven select committees into permanent "standing" committees, to handle legislation on an ongoing basis and oversee various executive departments.

The Civil War bought new emergencies, demanding expansion of the federal spending process. In 1867, the Senate created the Appropriations Committee, which oversees all federal funding. Until then, the Finance Committee handled most appropriations, which meant that senators who pushed a given project through committee approval also oversaw approval of its funding—a recipe for carelessness and abuse.

Other committees came later, some fairly recently. In the

1970s, the Church Committee investigated abuses against Americans by U.S. investigative agencies, leading to the creation of intelligence committees.

For a time, committees sprouted to the point that in 1906 the Senate had sixty-six standing and select committees—more, by six, than it had majority-party members. According to the Senate historians, many committees and committee chairmanships developed solely to provide office space in the days before the first Senate Office Building opened. At least one committee never reviewed a bill or held a meeting. By 1920, the Senate had eighty committees, including the Committee on the Disposition of Useless Papers in the Executive Departments, and the Committee on Revolutionary War Claims—still going 137 years after the American Revolutionary War ended. But by 1920, senators all had private offices in the Senate Office Building and the country was in a post–World War I mood to modernize government. The Senate abolished forty-two obsolete committees.

In earlier eras, committee chairmen built and wielded enormous power. Senators took committee gavels by seniority, and generally kept them once they got them. That approach brought expertise and skilled leadership to committee helms, but it also carried drawbacks. In the first half of the twentieth century, entrenched Democrats, perpetually reelected in single-party Southern states, chaired the bulk of Senate committees and assured, among other dynamics, that no civil rights bill passed.

Changes in the process for appointing committee chairmen, away from a strict seniority system, reduced some of the chairs' power. Term limits took away more. In 1997, Senate Republicans imposed six-year term limits on their committee and subcommittee chairs. The change gave younger members a chance to lead committees, but also deprived the Senate and the country of expert, experienced committee chairmen.[1]

Even if committee chairmen have lost some of their might, most senators will not cross the leader of a committee on which they sit. As a shrewd staff director told Matthews: "Challenging the power of the chairman is not done because it doesn't pay off. There's no percentage in it. He could make a committee member's life miserable and futile for a long, long time."[2]

For an administration, working effectively and cooperatively with Senate committees and their chairman is key to passing legislation. Let's look at the two recent attempts at comprehensive health care reform, first by the Clinton administration in the early 1990s and then by the Obama administration from 2009 to 2010. In each case, congressional leaders told the administration to produce a bill, which they did. President and Mrs. Clinton argued that the Congress would never be able to agree on a draft for comprehensive health care reform—which historical records substantiate. The problem was, the administration could have been much more collaborative in the drafting stages. Resulting delays in drafting a bill gave opponents time to mobilize and spread their message, while a series of foreign crises hurt the president's popularity. In the end, the Clinton health care effort never got a Senate vote. Majority Leader George Mitchell, knowing he didn't have the votes to pass the measure, pulled the bill.

By the time President Obama was elected in 2008, the conventional wisdom was that the Clintons had made a mistake in the 1990s by handing a detailed health care bill to Congress and telling members to pass it. The Obama administration was determined to turn over the writing of the actual bill to Congress. Many congressional leaders were very frustrated that the president didn't provide more guidance and wasn't more forceful about many of the key issues.

Obama could have been more assertive and could have given more hands-on direction as the draft was being negotiated.

Turning the effort completely over to Congress was chaotic, uncontrolled, and far too long in the writing. Obama wanted to let the Senate leaders and committee chairmen do their jobs, without embarrassing them by pressuring them publicly. But he did not walk away from the process. Behind the scenes, where much of the legislative action takes place, the president was talking daily to the Finance Committee chairman and constantly to Democratic leaders about the need to get moving. Still, Obama's "go fast" strategy derailed, as the Clinton effort had also badly missed self-imposed deadlines. And while the Obama administration and congressional leaders made substantial public pushes for the bill, a lack of persistent engagement, cajoling, and direction nearly killed the second major effort for health care reform.

Finding the right balance between being deferential to congressional leadership and providing strong presidential leadership is a huge challenge. My own view is that the ideal drafting environment for something as complex as health care legislation was somewhere between the Clinton and Obama approaches.

☆ 20. SENATE RULES ☆

President Calvin Coolidge quipped, "I soon found that the Senate had but one fixed rule . . . which was to the effect that the Senate would do anything it wanted to do whenever it wanted to do it."

The Senate runs by complex procedures—codified by the Senate itself, but also driven by precedent and custom—that can expedite, delay, or kill measures. Senators can also exploit the rules for stagecraft and artifice, such as opposing the debate procedure on a bill they don't like, rather than objecting to the underlying bill itself, to avoid going on record against the bill's substance.

Many of the Senate's rules are unwritten, and senators routinely agree to waive the relatively few standing rules, to move things along. Rules in the Senate, an institution of individuals, stress minority rights, extended debate, and amendments. One senator can bring the whole body to a halt. As Mondale put it, "When majorities prevail in the Senate, it is only by leave of minorities . . ."[1]

The Senate's rules make it hard to pass anything without

overwhelming support. Today's hyperpolarization and gridlock make the Senate essentially a sixty-vote, or "supermajority" body.

Senate floor debate can look like an act from an antebellum drama. Senators use nineteenth-century language, following elaborate procedures and convoluted rules obtuse to anybody not steeped in them. But there's a purpose behind all of it.

Senate rules require members to address the presiding officer, never each other. They can't criticize another senator's state, or question a colleague's motives. If they do, they can be forced to sit down and sit out the debate. The result is dialogue that can seem quaint, stilted, and sometimes plain odd. A senator might say, "The distinguished senior senator from the great state of such and such is totally incorrect on this issue, and doesn't know what he's talking about."[2]

The formal language goes back to Thomas Jefferson, who while vice president drafted a manual of parliamentary procedure for the Senate. Jefferson reasoned that issues for debate could be so emotional and divisive that the only way to assure rational discussion was to deal with them politely. Remember, this is in a body where, as Matthews wrote, "Senators as a group are ambitious and egocentric men [and women], chosen through an electoral battle in which a talent for invective, righteous indignation, 'mud-slinging,' and 'engaging in personalities' are often assets."[3] The formal language, essentially, is a form of protection, or "linguistic lubrication," as one person called it.

Some decades ago, then-Majority Leader Alben Barkley advised a freshman senator, "If you think a colleague is stupid, refer to him as 'the able, learned and distinguished Senator,' but if you know he is stupid, refer to him as 'the *very* able, learned and distinguished Senator.'"[4]

Once a senator is recognized—and the presiding officer must recognize any senator who wishes to speak—that senator may hold the floor for as long as he or she wishes. These days, though, key debate plays out mostly behind the scenes, and floor statements seldom sway senators. Floor debate is rarely debate in the classic sense of an exchange of ideas aimed at persuading an opponent. In addition, stagecraft plays a large part. Senators often rail at an empty or near-empty chamber as though lecturing throngs of colleagues.

Today, senators often aim their floor speeches at the public, their supporters, and the folks back home. Their press offices routinely send transcripts and video clips to local media and post them on their Web sites. Also, many speeches and other comment on the floor are designed to explain the legislation for legislative history purposes and later legal interpretation. They're also designed to inform the executive branch of the intent of certain provisions for both regulatory and implementation purposes.

Senate rules may be complex, but you need to master them to be an effective legislator, or opponents will take advantage of you. New senators should listen carefully when the parliamentarian—a neutral expert always available on the floor—explains a Senate rule. You learn gradually and then, like studying a foreign language, you build enough of a base and it all comes together.

Most often, though, the rules are set aside by unanimous consent, or "UC," in favor of more streamlined procedures. Otherwise, the Senate would get bogged down by its massive workload. A UC might cover routine business such as asking to print a speech in the *Congressional Record* as though it had been delivered on the floor, or it might set terms of debate and types of amendments allowed on a given bill. A UC might skip the required three readings of a bill, which could take hours—and does, when senators insist on it as delaying tactic. That's why you occasionally hear Senate clerks intoning legislative language, taking turns in order to save their voices as they read hundreds of pages aloud.

In the individual-centered institution that is the U.S. Senate, the unanimous consent process requires just that—unanimous consent. Any senator can object to a UC, stymieing legislation and slowing or stopping the entire Senate.

Republican Leader Robert Taft quipped: "I have yet to discover how an ordinary Senator ever gets a bill though if one other Senator objects. Apparently all legislation is by unanimous consent or physical exhaustion."

Walter Oleszek, a Library of Congress expert on congressional procedures and policy, gave me some exaggerated credit on page one of his widely used textbook for outmaneuvering one of the greatest masters of the Senate rules, Robert Byrd:

In the Senate, procedures are designed to emphasize extended deliberation over expedited decision making. In October 2002, however, Senate Majority Leader Tom Daschle, D-S.D., hastened a vote on a consequential joint resolution authorizing President George W. Bush to launch a preemptive military strike against Iraq. Daschle did so by taking procedural action to limit the possibility of any filibuster (or extended debate) on the issue . . . But Sen. Robert C. Byrd, D-W.Va., a master of parliamentary procedure, made it clear to the other senators that he wanted to discuss the Iraq resolution at length . . . Unhappily, Byrd witnessed the majority leader use Senate rules against him. Daschle invoked a procedure called cloture, or "closure" of debate, to end any chance for lengthy discussion of the Iraq resolution. Furthermore, when word circulated that Byrd might resort to delaying tactics, such as engaging in a talkathon on the preamble to the joint resolution, the majority leader "responded by moving the preamble into the main text, preempting such a move by Byrd. And he did it after the senator and others had left for the evening."[5] . . . In the end, after five days of debate, the Senate granted Bush authority to launch preemptive military action against Iraq.[6]

With the benefit of hindsight, given the debacle in Iraq, I should have given Senator Byrd all the time he needed.

☆ 21. QUORUMS ☆

The Senate cannot conduct business unless a majority of its members, or a "quorum," is in the chamber. In 1789, the first senators needed weeks to gather a quorum. On March 4, 1789, eight senators arrived in the new nation's temporary capital in New York City to open the first Congress. By then, eleven states had ratified the Constitution, so the Senate needed twelve of its twenty-two members for a quorum. The eight senators who had shown up wrote to the others, "earnest[ly] requesting that you will be so obliging as to attend as soon as possible." Finally, after more than a month, the twelfth senator arrived on April 6. The Senate then took up its first order of business—certifying George Washington's election as president, five weeks after Washington's term had officially begun.

These days, the Senate routinely operates with fewer than fifty-one members on the floor. Except during votes, only a few members are usually in the chamber. A quorum is always assumed to be present, unless a senator objects.

Watching floor debate, you'll often hear a senator say, "Mr. President, I note the absence of a quorum" or "Madam President, I suggest the absence of a quorum." Then the presiding officer may direct the clerk to "call the roll," or to take attendance, as your kindergarten teacher might have done.

Most of these are "routine quorum calls," which are not actually intended to summon senators to the floor. Rather, they are useful devices to suspend formal floor action, to buy senators time to informally work out compromise amendments or to hold private talks, to give a scheduled speaker or floor manager more time to arrive, or when there is no one to speak on the floor or the Senate is between legislative work and doesn't want to recess or adjourn. The clerk generally reads the roll slowly, and routine quorum calls can run more than an hour. Senators can end the quorum call simply by agreeing to a unanimous consent request to rescind it before the clerk finishes the roster.

A "live quorum call," however, *is* intended to muster a majority of members to the floor. The Majority Leader may announce that a quorum call is live because he wants senators on the floor for any of a variety of reasons. Senate rules require live quorum calls right before a cloture vote and before the Senate acts on a unanimous consent request to set a date for voting on a bill or joint resolution, but senators can waive those requirements by unanimous consent, and often do.

If the clerk finishes reading the roll and a majority of senators has not reported, the Senate cannot resume its legislative business. Nor can it end the quorum call, since it has established the absence of a quorum.

Senators sometimes strategically avoid the floor, to deny a quorum and with it the chance to move a measure they oppose. The Framers anticipated such tactics. The Constitution authorizes both the House and Senate to "compel the Attendance of absent Members, in such Manner, and under such Penalties as each House may provide."

The Senate created the office of sergeant at arms to track down truant senators and reluctant witnesses. In 1798, the Senate passed a rule allowing less than a quorum of senators to authorize the sergeant at arms to haul back their absent colleagues to the chamber. That year, more than one in three senators had left the Capitol early, many heading home for the five-month recess. Those senators who had left without a satisfactory excuse had to pay whatever expenses the sergeant at arms ran up in bringing them back.

In 1987, Senate Republicans filibustered over campaign finance reform. Bob Dole, then Minority Leader, mustered Senate Republicans in their cloakroom around 2 a.m. and told them to stay off the Senate floor. They scattered. Robert Byrd, then Minority Leader, made a motion to arrest absent senators. Sergeant at Arms Henry Giugni began patrolling the halls. The first truant senator that Giugni found, at about 3:30 a.m., was Lowell Weicker of Connecticut. Giugni was about five-feet-nine inches. Weicker was a hulking six-feet-four and 240 pounds, and tough. Prudently, Giugni decided not to arrest Weicker. Instead, he began knocking on senators' doors. Bob Packwood of Oregon answered, perhaps unwisely. Packwood, a middleweight, was then carried feet first into the Senate chamber.[1]

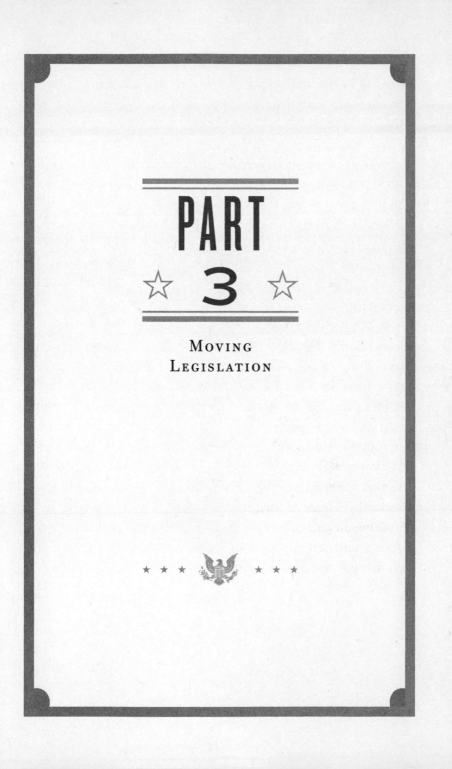

PART

☆ 3 ☆

MOVING
LEGISLATION

★ ★ ★ ★ ★ ★

22. INTRODUCING LEGISLATION

The nineteenth-century German Chancellor Otto von Bismarck said that laws are like sausages; it is better not to see them being made. Congress makes our federal laws through a complex process that demands strategy, tactics, timing, persuasion, pressure, bargaining—and sometimes luck.

While many use the term "bill" as a catch-all for any legislative proposal, a bill is actually only the most common of four types of legislation. A resolution covers matters in one chamber of Congress only, such as changes to that chamber's rules or procedures, or expressing the sense of the Senate on a public policy matter, and does not require approval by the other chamber or by the president, and does not carry the weight of law. A concurrent resolution covers administrative matters, such as Congress's adjournment date, and requires approval from both chambers of Congress to pass, but does not go to the president, and thus does not carry the weight of law. A joint resolution is essentially equivalent to a bill, but is generally used for limited, specific matters, such as a proposed amendment to the Constitution. We'll deal almost solely with bills, but it's important to note the other species within the genus.

Generally, senators and their staffs develop a bill's substance and work with the nonpartisan Office of Legislative Counsel to draft the legislation in proper form. Sometimes others, including advocacy groups and the White House, provide input on a bill's concepts and even its language.

A snappy title, such as the Dream Act, for a bill to provide citizenship to certain immigrants, or the Patriot Act, for a bill to enhance the government's ability to confront terrorism, can help a bill draw attention and support. Senators often go through contortions to contrive memorable acronyms for bill titles. The USA Patriot Act actually stands for: Uniting (and) Strengthening America (by) Providing Appropriate Tools Required (to) Intercept (and) Obstruct Terrorism.

A senator submits the bill to a clerk, or may introduce it on the floor. In addition to its name, every bill gets a number, corresponding to the order in which it was introduced during the particular Congress. While early numbers are generally reserved for the leadership, senators often try to claim a particular bill number, sometimes the same number for a bill they introduce repeatedly over various Congresses. Like titles, a memorable number can help a bill's prospects. Generally, a bill is referred to the appropriate standing committee, which will decide whether to report it to the full Senate for consideration.

Each Congress, senators introduce thousands of bills, but debate only a few dozen of them. Only a small fraction of the measures introduced, fewer than 4 percent, ultimately become law. Most bills, in fact, are introduced with no expectation that they will be enacted; their sponsors just want to make a statement or get a process started. Other bills are noncontroversial, such as "commemoratives" to rename a local post office or federal building, and usually sail through.

To increase chances of passage, senators seek cosponsors, circulating Dear Colleague letters that ask other senators to endorse their legislation. As a result, many senators announce their positions on a bill before it is even introduced, much less debated. At the extreme, the Vietnam War Memorial bill drew one hundred sponsors and cosponsors; the entire Senate had approved the measure before it even reached the floor.

Since any bill must pass the House and Senate in identical form before it can be sent for the president's signature, senators and House members often find a supporter in the other chamber to introduce a "companion bill," essentially the same legislation, so that each chamber can consider the measure at the same time, rather than waiting for one body to pass a bill before beginning the approval process on the measure in the other body.

Most senators arrive with high hopes of being involved in big legislative challenges. Virtually every senator is involved in efforts to address one or more of the major policy challenges our country faces. The problem has always been finding a consensus on these issues. That's why it took so long to pass comprehensive health care reform, for example, and why, arguably, we have never passed comprehensive energy policy. The Senate winds up devoting most of its deliberations to controversial major bills, which involve conflicting political needs and invite personality clashes and ideological battles. Congress works smoothest when it passes small, easily understood and popular measures.

Any given piece of legislation must pass during the two-year

Congress in which it is introduced, or it dies when that Congress adjourns. The final weeks of every congressional session see a flurry of bill introductions and action. A bill passes through more than one hundred specific steps from introduction to enactment[1], and many of those steps offer opportunities to delay, alter, or kill the measure.

23. HOLDS AND FILIBUSTERS

☆ ☆

Scheduling legislation, nominations or other measures for votes poses a huge challenge, because any one senator can put a "hold" on a bill. There's a lot of misunderstanding about what a hold is, so let's clear that up first. A hold is simply a threat of a filibuster. It's just a matter of a senator telling leadership that if you take up this bill or nomination, I'm going to filibuster. It's a signal to the leader that if they try to do something by unanimous consent, somebody will object.

As former Majority Leader Byrd said, "The leader is the prisoner of Senators, and always has been. Any Senator can object to time agreements, they can make it difficult for every other Senator."[1]

The Senate rules do not authorize holds. But party leaders would prefer knowing beforehand that a senator is going to object to a measure, rather than getting blindsided on the floor. It's important for the leaders to know, if they're going to ask for unanimous consent, that they're going to get it, or they're not. While Leaders sometimes tolerate holds, I spent a lot of time talking senators off their holds. Sometimes it requires a great deal of negotiation. And, of course, the ultimate tool to break a hold is a successful cloture motion. Generally, the Majority Leader won't call up a given matter until a hold has been lifted. So the hold becomes a quick, private, painless way for a senator to kill or delay Senate action.

The Senate has grappled for decades with holds, and especially with their secrecy. Senators want to know who is holding up their measure and why; if they knew, maybe they could chat with that person, said Walter Oleszek, the congressional procedures and policy expert. Many senators now publicize their holds, announcing them in the *Congressional Record*, Oleszek said, because it gives them leverage and they want people to come to them, including the administration.[2]

Bipartisan reform efforts in 2007 and 2011 to place time limitations on holds have made the practice more difficult and reduced it, but it still endures. To evade the new rules, senators often use rolling holds, which are like tag-team tactics in which one senator places a hold on a bill for a number of days, and then lifts it as another senator places a hold.[3]

Sometimes a hold can be accommodated; it's not necessarily designed to kill the measure. A senator may just want the nominee to come talk to him, or want an amendment considered for a bill. In June 2003, an Idaho senator placed a hold on promotions of more than two hundred Air Force officers, solely to press the Air Force to base four new cargo planes in his state, a commitment the senator claimed that the Air Force had made to him years earlier. There has been a real abuse of the hold process in recent years. Virtually all bills today are subject to holds. Unfortunately, my experience was that more often than not, talking to a senator did little good.

Unless you eliminate the filibuster itself, you're always going to have holds. The question becomes whether these notices—which, again, are useful—should be made public. I've come to the conclusion that they should be.

There's also a lot of misperception about what a filibuster is. Let's clear that up, too. The public concept of the filibuster comes largely from Hollywood, with a single senator seizing the floor for hours, talking himself hoarse and finally passing out, as Jimmy Stewart did in Frank Capra's 1939 classic film, *Mr. Smith Goes to Washington*.

Some senators actually have waged such talkathons, though not recently. Strom Thurmond still holds the record at 24 hours and 18 minutes for his leg of a filibuster against the Civil Rights Act of 1957. Thurmond finally yielded after doctors threatened to yank him from the floor over concern about kidney damage.

But a filibuster really is any tactic to prevent the majority from ever getting to a vote, on the assumption that if the majority could vote, it would prevail. So more often than not, a filibuster involves voting against a cloture motion, or objecting to a unanimous consent agreement, which doesn't require any speech at all, other than "I object." In short, a filibuster—which comes from the Dutch word for freebooter, or pirate—involves using the rules of the Senate to slow things and to frustrate the majority. Holds are part of all that.

Every one of these tactics empowers every single senator, even the greenest freshman. In the House, you have to join a huge group to wield such power, such as a big freshman class or a state delegation or a caucus, or spend decades amassing enough seniority to chair a committee and get some heft. In the Senate, you get that power the minute you take the oath of office.

_____

Beginning in the late nineteenth century, senators pressed, without success, to pass a rule limiting debate. By 1915, while the conflict that would become World War I raged in Europe, the Senate was facing an epidemic of filibusters, blocking action on vital measures including major appropriations bills. In 1917, a twenty-three-day filibuster against President Woodrow Wilson's proposal to arm merchant ships against German submarine attacks killed a host of other vital bills.

Facing a wartime crisis, Wilson railed that the "Senate of the United States is the only legislative body in the world which cannot act when its majority is ready for action. A little group of willful men, representing no opinion but their own, have rendered the great government of the United States helpless and contemptible." Wilson demanded that the Senate adopt a cloture rule, to allow for cutting off debate. In 1885, Wilson had written his doctoral thesis at Johns Hopkins, "Congressional Government," on the federal government, especially the U.S. Senate. He aspired to be a senator. Ironically, in the dissertation, he asserted that Senate tradition and practice argued against implementing a rule on cloture.

In March 1917, in a special congressional session, the Senate agreed to a rule that allowed a two-thirds majority to end debate, but also allowed each senator to speak for an additional hour after invoking cloture but before voting on final passage of the given bill. Over the next forty-six years, the Senate invoked cloture only five times. Southern senators, in particular, exploited filibusters to block civil rights legislation, including antilynching and polling bills, until the Senate invoked cloture after a fifty-seven day filibuster against the Civil Rights Act of 1964. In 1975, the Senate reduced the number of votes required for cloture to three fifths from two thirds, or a more manageable sixty of the one hundred senators. Invoking cloture would now also limit debate to thirty hours.

In recent decades, the number of filibusters has skyrocketed. For most of the twentieth century, we averaged single digits. Now, we're up to well over a hundred in a Congress, over fifty in a year. In other words, we've gone from maybe one a month to one a week. More cloture petitions have been filed in the last five years than in the seventy years from 1917 to 1986, when a reform approach called dual-tracking began. And there were many twentieth-century Congresses in which no cloture petitions were filed at all. Several factors contributed.

First, dual-tracking let the Senate just set aside an embattled bill and take up something else. The idea was, at least you'd use time on the Senate floor for great value, or greater value. The problem is, offering a legislative escape just makes filibusters all the more common; if you don't pay any price for the filibuster, it's much easier to use.

Dual-tracking has also further reduced the full-throated filibuster, now rare, of *Mr. Smith Goes to Washington* fame. We no longer ask people to hold the floor while they're filibustering, and thus no longer need to keep in other senators around the clock.

Also, filibusters have become powerful leverage devices. Since a party rarely commands sixty votes in the Senate, straight party-line votes won't overcome a filibuster, or generally pass controversial legislation. The Senate's institutional checks on the majority have long made it easier for a minority to block initiatives than for a majority to pass them. Even with the 1975 reform, proponents need a sixty-vote "supermajority" to invoke cloture and force a final vote on a bill, while opponents need only forty-one votes to continue debate and delay a vote.

The condensed Senate workweek has added further leverage to the filibuster. Senators' now near-universal practice of spending weekends in their home states has effectively shortened the workweek to Tuesday through Thursday. The short time to get anything done has made the threat of filibuster more potent, though the sixty-vote requirement to do business forces compromise and bipartisanship. Well, sometimes.

So the filibuster, aided by its cousin the hold, has now become the most effective leverage device in a closely divided Senate, almost accepted as common practice. A senator who knows the leader isn't going to spend the time to win supermajorities to clear votes on a motion to proceed, and then on the underlying bill, and on amendments to the bill, has several options for filibusters on any given measure.

The filibuster is abused terribly today, especially on nominations. The president's selections for key positions get held up for years at a time. Filibusters against nominees can keep executive agencies and courts across the country understaffed, and create a chilling effect that keeps top talent from even accepting nominations.

In recent decades, when the party out of the White House controlled the Senate, judicial nominees in particular have faced filibusters or other legislative delays, in an escalating tit-for-tat under the Payback Theory. The issue came to a head in November 2003, when four of President George W. Bush's appeals court nominees faced filibusters, and Republicans launched a Justice for Judges Marathon, a talkathon to draw attention to their cause.

Republicans laid out ten cots in the Strom Thurmond Room, near the Senate floor, so they could man the debate at all hours. Some found it ironic that Republicans used the Thurmond Room, named for the late South Carolina Republican who still holds the filibuster record, over a civil rights bill. Democrats would not need cots for the marathon, I told *Congressional Quarterly*. "We're tougher than they are."[4]

In the hours before the debate began, as *Congressional Quarterly* described it, "the Senate side of the Capitol was transformed into a media circus, with photographers and reporters moving from one staged news event to another." Each side set up "war rooms" to host news conferences and give interviews.

Republicans showed charts, some featuring photos of the nominees being filibustered, which *The New York Times* described as resembling posters of missing children. Then-Senator Hillary Clinton unveiled a huge chart showing 168 apples and 4 lemons, representing President Bush's 168 judges who had been confirmed and the four that were being blocked. Republicans griped that the lemons were a gratuitous insult to the nominees. Both sides acknowledged that the event was mostly about stirring their bases and raising money.

In the end, the marathon did not generate the furor of interest Republicans had sought, and that the general issue of blocked nominees genuinely deserved. *The New York Times* wrote: "The extraordinary session . . . was more than anything a vivid demonstration of the decline in relations between the two parties."[5]

24. MOVING LEGISLATION

⭐ ⭐

In a legislative landscape fraught with holds, filibusters, and other obstacles, how do you strategically advance a bill?

As Majority Leader, I instituted standing Wednesday lunches with my committee chairmen. We would talk over what legislation really needed to be brought to the floor, and how long debate would take. We'd go around the table, and each would report what was going on and what he or she thought I needed to know. Those sessions provided my best intelligence about the legislative agenda and the status of bills working their way through. The lunches also gave me an opportunity to persuade any recalcitrant chairs. If one chairman was reluctant to advance a measure I considered necessary, all the other chairs could help persuade him or her that the effort was worthwhile.

Then you also have to work with the Minority Leader, who is very instrumental in making it either easier or harder to get bills onto the floor. As historian Ritchie put it:

With rules that foster deliberation, cooperation and consensus building, the majority cannot relegate the minority to the role of bystanders. The majority leader sets the agenda by calling bills from the calendar, but the minority leader holds an arsenal of parliamentary weapons for blocking action. Little of consequence happens in the Senate, therefore, unless the two party leaders have reached some accord. Even then, dissenters from either party can derail their efforts . . . [1]

Often, advancing a bill involves recognizing the minority's need to offer certain amendments. So leaders would set agreements regarding amendments that would be offered, including the time for debating them.

After all the intelligence gathering, persuasion, strategy, and tactics, moving legislation involves a significant amount of negotiation, and even then you can't guarantee how long consideration will take. We once worked on an energy bill for nearly three months, on and off the floor, until we finally got it passed.

25. THE POLITICS OF INCLUSION

Accomplishing much in the Senate—and in life—generally requires cooperation and teamwork. I have always believed in the politics of inclusion, consensus, coalition building, connection. After all, the Senate, at its core, is a complex web of relationships—a hundred men and women from different backgrounds, beliefs, points of view, experiences, abilities, all thrown together to make the laws of the land, with six years to prove themselves. They all have their own obligations to both the nation as a whole and to their individual states and constituencies.

The Senate is about creating alliances. The only way you can bring together such a disparate collection of individuals into a majority for a vote on any given issue is to understand what drives them, what angers them, what approach works with them, and ultimately what can convince them to join with you.

A senator must be a student of human nature. As Majority Leader Baker said, "What really makes the Senate work—as our heroes knew profoundly—is an understanding of human nature . . . of one's colleagues and one's constituents."[1]

This approach requires, above all, the ability to listen, to consider, and to try to incorporate another person's viewpoint. Listening isn't as simple as some may think. As Judiciary Chairman Patrick Leahy said, "There's a difference between just being quiet and actually listening."

Days after President Obama's inauguration, he told me during a meeting about health care that he had listened to economic advisors argue for delaying the initiative, even though the president considered it more important than ever, because he wanted to hear all sides of the debate. The president told me that we shared a trait; we both strived to be good listeners. Good listening is the mark of good, open-minded leadership. Secretary of State Dean Rusk once said that "the best way to persuade is with your ears."

Government is always better when its leaders hear as many points of view as possible, and gather ideas from the widest possible range of people who will be affected by their decisions.

Preparation and paying attention also go a long way in building legislative alliances. By paying attention, I mean not only listening to people, but also trying to understand them. Senators have to divine their colleagues' individual temperaments and wills. This ability is at the root of building coalitions and achieving consensus.

Understanding means putting yourself in other people's shoes—including your opponents'—to get a sense of what it feels like to *be* them. No matter how you feel about another person, it's always in your best interest to empathize, in order to understand. Often, this process can shape and shift your opinion, and theirs. Politics, some say, is the art of persuasion. There's no better way to persuade than to show others that you understand what *they* need, not just what *you* need.

In the Senate, you need to understand not just *what* the other person says or believes, which can be hard enough, but *why*.

If a senator lines up against you, it's just as important to understand why, because in the Senate every debate, vote, and political battle is a prelude to the next one. An opponent in today's fight may well become an ally in tomorrow's, if you can shape an understanding of that person that serves as the foundation of a relationship.

You can sometimes find common ground in unexpected places. As the old saying goes, "Politics makes strange bedfellows." That doesn't just mean officials with different points of view who find a narrow mutual interest. Sometimes strong friendships develop between two senators of opposite parties from the same state because they'll never run against each other, the way the election cycles go, and they don't tap the same funding sources or address the same audiences, although they do compete for media attention. Meanwhile, the most difficult relationships at times arise between two senators of the same party from the same state, appealing to the same supporters.

26. LEADING *AND* REPRESENTING

☆ ☆

In the republic's early days, senators often received letters of instruction from the state legislatures that appointed them. They could follow the instructions, and often did with fanfare, ignore them at their peril, or resign.

In October 1795, the *Kentucky Gazette* printed a petition from the people of Clark County to their state legislature denouncing their U.S. senator, Humphrey Marshall, for voting to ratify a controversial treaty, and urging the legislature to instruct Marshall to oppose the treaty if it came before the Senate again. Marshall penned a series of articles to explain his ratification vote directly to the people. He stated that he was more interested in doing his duty to the nation "according to my own judgment" than in winning popularity contests. Soon afterward, a mob dragged Marshall from his house and nearly threw him into the Kentucky River. Angry Kentuckians stoned him in the state capital. Marshall kept a low profile for the rest of his term.

Americans continue to urge their senators to cast particular votes or introduce particular bills, sometimes in strong terms. And that's how it should be. But senators go to Washington to do more than blindly follow their constituents' orders. They must also lead.

In the Senate, many choices are difficult and complex, as competing proposals vie for finite federal resources, especially today when we face a mounting national debt. And constituents are hardly the only group that exerts pressure. Senators also regularly face pressure from colleagues, party leaders, the president or executive branch, interest groups, and the media.

In the end, a senator must serve as a combination of representative and leader, delegate and trustee. People used to ask me, "So what are the bases, the criteria you use to make your decision on a given bill?" There are several:

1. What do my constituents feel? But oftentimes, letter-writing or call-in campaigns are orchestrated—more Astroturf than grass roots—so you can't just take the volume of mail and phone calls you get as a measure of the sentiment of the people you represent.
2. What is the best expert advice you can get on a given issue? Is there an expert consensus?
3. Your own judgment—what are your values, what is your judgment, what do you think is the right thing to do? Instinctively, intellectually, or ideologically, what's in your heart? What's in your gut? You have a responsibility to use your best judgment.

The more directly a matter affects the voters, particularly on economic policy, the more constituents expect their representatives to exercise their instructions. Voters usually show greater tolerance of a senator's independence on more indirect issues, such as national defense and foreign policy. But making decisions is often tough, in any policy area. Highlighting just how tough it can be to defy constituents' wishes to do what you believe is right, and how high a price you may pay, then-Senator John F. Kennedy profiled eight senators who had taken such heroic actions in his 1956 Pulitzer Prize–winning book, *Profiles in Courage*.

Among his eight heroes, Kennedy featured Daniel Webster for supporting the Compromise of 1850, a set of five bills on the spread of slavery to U.S. territories, designed to balance northern and Southern interests and keep the nation together. The Fugitive Slave Act was the package's most controversial measure, requiring the return of escaped slaves and denying a fugitive's right to a jury trial.

Webster began his famous Seventh of March speech, "Mr. President, I wish to speak today, not as a Massachusetts man, nor as a Northern man, but as an American, and a member of the Senate of the United States. . . . I speak for the preservation of the Union. Hear me for my cause."

Webster won plaudits for moral courage nearly everywhere except in his base of New England, where he was reviled, with abolitionists calling him a traitor or worse. He soon resigned from the Senate. Former President Ford captured the drama and import of Webster's action:

> At a critical moment in the nation's history, when disunion loomed and popular democracy itself was threatened with extinction, Webster faced an excruciating choice. Here, within these very walls, he looked into his political grave.
>
> . . . Webster's cause was the Compromise of 1850. Like most compromises, it was easier to criticize than to embrace. . . . However unpopular his action might have been at the time, Webster helped to delay the Civil War for a

decade. As a result, the chances were vastly increased that when war did come, it would forever eradicate the stain of slavery from American soil.[1]

Presidents can also apply strong pressure on senators. President Clinton's late-night phone calls are legendary, and I got more than my share of them, usually when we were launching a bill and shaping strategy. Typically, a president gets involved at such intensity with his own party when a piece of legislation is being prepared. As the bill makes its way toward a vote, he'll keep weighing in. Finally, when a vote nears, the president will really start pushing, phoning undecided or hold-out senators on both sides of the aisle, inviting them to the Oval Office for a meeting, or even to the White House residential area, maybe for a meal.

Some executive-branch officials press senators even more directly for their votes. A week after the terrorist attacks of September 11, 2001, Attorney General John Ashcroft, a former senator, publicly demanded that within four days, Congress pass the Patriot Act, a collection of counterterrorism proposals designed to strengthen law enforcement's powers to investigate and catch suspected terrorists living in the United States. Ashcroft did not even provide a draft of the legislation to Congress for another two days, making the impossible demand even more unreal. Torturous negotiations on the legislation between White House and Senate staffers followed. Ultimately, in early October, I introduced a Senate alternative to the Ashcroft bill, with Republican Leader Lott as one of the prime cosponsors. A week later, the Senate passed the bill, and late that month, the president signed a final bill into law.

27. BUILDING COALITIONS

Building a majority coalition to pass a given piece of legislation presents an intriguing challenge. Coalitions generally require bipartisanship. You defeat your purpose if you try to find a coalition solely within your caucus. The best coalition oftentimes comes when the two Leaders themselves are on the same side. There are five significant components to coalition-building:

1. Building as broad a coalition as possible involves a recognition that the group has to include both Republicans and Democrats.
2. An effective coalition usually requires the support and involvement of outside groups. Those groups can include think tanks, advocacy groups, and constituents.
3. Coalitions involve *compromise*. You can't have it all your way, or you're not going to put that coalition together. You've got to make sure the coalition recognizes the need for common ground, which is the glue that keeps the components together.

4. A coalition that gets too far in the weeds will break apart. Coalitions are generally built around principles, not highly delineated specifics. It's easy to talk about a patients' bill of rights, or universal health care, or cost-containment. It's tougher to agree on the details, however. So oftentimes coalitions are built around issues at the thirty-thousand-foot level.

5. A strong coalition needs a strong message. What is your identifying mark? What is your characteristic? A coalition can have a name, which also advances its message. The bipartisan Senate Cancer Coalition advanced the fight against cancer partly by inviting advocates and scientists to testify at high-profile hearings.

The effort, beginning in the 1990s, to build a coalition on the Patients' Bill of Rights proved interesting, and instructive. Just the name said it all; rights for patients who were feeling disenfranchised by the health system. For a time, Senate coalition leaders included Ted Kennedy and John McCain, a high-profile bipartisan duo. And the cause was something that everybody at the time supported, given the many problems associated with managed care, a system in which a health maintenance organization (HMO) or other network acts as an intermediary between patients and their providers, generally restricting choice of providers and treatment options.

Sometimes help comes from unexpected quarters. The 1997 film *As Good as It Gets,* starring Jack Nicholson and Helen Hunt, featured a scene in which Hunt's character, the mother of a boy suffering from asthma and allergies, gets a house call from a doctor that Nicholson's curmudgeonly character has sent over. It becomes clear that the boy has not received key tests and treatments because Hunt's HMO didn't cover them, telling Hunt that such efforts were unnecessary. Hunt blares a string of profanities to describe HMOs, then says, "I'm sorry."

"It's okay," the kindly doctor says. "Actually, I think that's their technical name."

Across the country, theater audiences cheered, showing the depth of public feeling about managed care. People cited the film as one of the reasons for launching the Patients' Bill of Rights.

We tried several times to reach a coalition agreement. The health sector was deeply divided, concerned that the legislation would overly constrain them. If constituency groups are in opposition, that undermines your chances right out of the box to get a coalition. While Patients' Bill of Rights legislation did not immediately pass into law, the concerns that inspired the effort eventually spurred reforms, ultimately through the health care overhaul passed in 2010.

In building a Senate majority to pass a given piece of legislation, bargaining can play a key role. Senators and Senate leaders employ three main techniques: logrolling, compromise, and nonlegislative favors.

"Logrolling" involves senators' swapping support for different bills: you vote for this, I'll vote for that. Senators generally have different priorities, and a senator may be willing to trade his vote on a measure he doesn't feel strongly about for another senator's vote on a measure about which he cares deeply.

In a compromise, each side modifies its demands to make them more palatable to the other side, to reach a mutually acceptable middle ground. A good compromise, by one definition, leaves nobody happy. The easiest compromises to forge can involve funding bills, where the two sides split the difference.

Nonlegislative favors involve satisfying any of a host of goals that reluctant senators may have, beyond their policy agendas. A senator's goals might include winning assignment to a prestigious committee, raising campaign funds, running for higher office, or attending an overseas conference.[1] Senate leaders are best positioned to grant such favors. This tactic can be particularly effective in convincing a senator to withdraw a hold, as we discussed earlier.

Lyndon Johnson, as Majority Leader, was a master of the nonlegislative favor. As historian Doris Kearns Goodwin wrote:

> For Johnson, each one of these assignments contained a potential opportunity for bargaining, for creating obligations, provided that he knew his fellow senators well enough to determine which invitations would matter the most to whom. If he knew that the wife of the senator from Idaho had been dreaming of a trip to Paris for ten years, or that the advisers to another senator had warned him about his slipping popularity with Italian voters, Johnson could increase the potential usefulness of assignments to the Parliamentary Conference in Paris or to the dedication of the cemeteries in Italy."[2]

Moving legislation has been called "the art of the doable." Ted Kennedy was another master, despite his reputation as a die-hard, intractable liberal. Kennedy understood that you can't always get all you want, and that sometimes it's better to settle for all you *can* get rather than fighting to the bitter end and ending up with nothing. In that spirit, popular advice on Capitol Hill holds, "Don't let the perfect become the enemy of the good."

In 2001, after nearly six months of negotiations on the No Child Left Behind bill, Ted Kennedy and the George W. Bush White House finally reached agreement. Democratic senators involved in drafting the bill met in a Capitol room across the hall from my office. In keeping with my approach, I invited each of the dozen or so senators to express their views on the draft bill. The moderates joined Kennedy in arguing that we had made great progress in negotiating many of the issues with the Bush administration. The liberals, while acknowledging that progress, argued that we had still failed to lock in the necessary resources to help schools correct the deficiencies that the testing would certainly reveal.

After listening to both sides, and after a great deal of thought, I said that my heart was with those pushing for the resources, but my head was with those who felt we ought to lock in the accomplishments we'd made and continue to work on the resources. With that, the meeting ended.[3]

Leading a coalition, like leading the Senate, is the equivalent of loading frogs in a wheelbarrow. The frogs jump out of the coalition wheelbarrow pretty quickly. It's a fragile organizational entity, to say the least. A bipartisan coalition of senators dedicated to solving the debt-reduction morass in 2011 was given the name the Gang of Six, and for a time became the Gang of Five.

The 1999 Senate trial of President Clinton offers one of the better illustrations of how coalition building can make a profound difference in the workings of the Senate. In December 1998, the Republican-controlled House of Representatives impeached Clinton on charges of perjury and obstruction of justice, stemming from his alleged involvement with a White House intern, as detailed through an independent counsel's expansive investigation. Under the Constitution, it fell to the Republican-controlled Senate to try the president. Under the Constitution, a two-thirds majority was required to convict.

As the trial was about to begin, there were many differences of opinion in the Senate and many different ideas on how we should proceed. This was only the second time in history that a president had been impeached, and the first time in more than a hundred years, since the Senate tried Andrew Johnson in 1868.

Trent Lott and I convened the only joint caucus ever held of all one hundred senators. We called the meeting in the Old Senate Chamber, where Webster had made his Seventh of March speech, where Clay and Calhoun had battled. We wanted to give the occasion gravitas; to create a profoundly historic and momentous feel to what we were about to undertake. We needed folding chairs for forty senators because the chamber had seats for only sixty-four—which was why the Senate had left the grand old room back in the mid-nineteenth century.

We asked Senator Robert Byrd, the former Majority Leader and a gifted historian, to open by giving us an historical perspective, and he delivered a riveting history of impeachments. Then we invited every senator to speak on the issue.

When we began discussing procedure, we knew we would need to resolve some very difficult differences of opinion. At one point, Ted Kennedy made some recommendations and Phil Gramm (R-Texas), of all people, agreed, but then had his own ideas on what the procedure should be. If Kennedy was the Senate's quintessential liberal, Gramm was a conservative's conservative. Both were Senate titans.

Kennedy and Gramm reached essentially the same conclusion, that we didn't have enough agreement to write the trial rules to get to home plate, but that we had enough agreement to write the rules to get to second base. So let's write the rules to get to second base, they suggested, and when we get there, we can write the rules to get home. Cheers rang. We later voted 100–0 to move forward on developing a set of rules.

"The House floor managers were furious," Ritchie recalled, "because they thought that because their party controlled the Senate, they would write the rules to favor them. Instead, the rules were written as a neutral, fair set of rules. There was a lot of fallout on the House side on that; they referred to the Senate as Mount Olympus."[4]

We tasked Gramm and Kennedy to form a coalition to work out the final procedural questions. A lot of people over the years have remarked how unusual it was for those two, of all senators, to lead this coalition. But it saved the day. Their efforts allowed us to find a way forward and to find common ground.

Historian Ritchie credited the Senate for thinking and acting historically in the trial, compared to the House's more political approach in the impeachment.

> And as result, the trial was done very well. And even though most everybody knew what the outcome was going to be, they agreed that the trial proceeded in adult and appropriate manner, and that the Senate came off having done its job but also having looked well in the process.[5]

☆ 28. LOBBYISTS ☆

Interests across the gamut in America and around the world now spend billions of dollars a year to send thousands of registered lobbyists to plead their cases in Washington. On major issues, both sides deploy lobbyists.

Senate Democratic whip Dick Durbin, criticizing a banking bill, said on the Senate floor: "A friend of mine who is a lobbyist downtown in Washington said, 'Durbin, praise the Lord. Come up with some more ideas. This is a full-employment amendment. Everybody who is a lobbyist in Washington is working on this amendment. We just love you to pieces.'"[1]

Lobbyists do play a very important role, which has been buried in misconceptions. Contrary to conventional wisdom, lobbyists, or the groups they represent, are not all bad. They can help senators and their staffs understand issues and public views, and can help communicate senators' support to constituents. (Full disclosure: my wife is a very successful registered lobbyist.)

Ritchie called lobbyists "a legitimate part of the legislative process," noting that lobbyists know Congress, having sometimes served as legislators or congressional staff, and can offer expertise on specific issues and also advise Congress on what one lobbyist has called "economic and political realities."[2]

Oftentimes, lobbyists are extremely well informed. And good lobbyists, in presenting information, will put the material in the best light for their constituencies or clients, but will also be very honest with you. Anything less, and they won't maintain the relationships and reputations they depend on.

The relationship is symbiotic. A senator can give a lobbyist a chance to showcase his views and stature, for example, by slating him to testify at a committee hearing. Association chiefs sometimes plead with senators to testify at high-profile hearings on their issues.

The concept of lobbying goes to the heart of what representative democracy is all about. It's impractical, obviously, for all 300-million-plus Americans to descend on Washington to express their views. So over the years, groups have sought people, either on a paid or voluntary basis, who can articulate their points of view on given issues and circumstances. And that's as it should be. There should also be complete transparency, and there should be access in the process for those who don't have lobbyists.

Lobbying has soiled its name, however, through what has become a close and problematic correlation between contributions for political purposes and advocacy. The amount of money being raised and spent, and its role in the legislative process, is precarious—and it is getting worse. Political action committees, or PACs, groups that advocate for or against candidates or legislation, have been increasingly influencing elections, though they face contribution limits. The Supreme Court's *Citizens United v. Federal Election Commission* decision in 2010 now allows interests to form super PACs without limits on the amount of money they can raise; they can ask for millions of dollars from a single giver.

That is a destructive new aspect to political advocacy that we have to be very concerned about.

When the level of money becomes as consequential as it has, and the contributions to senators' reelection campaigns as large as they've grown, lobbyists can often influence decision making. Money is power, and we're seeing more of a concentration of power that comes as a result of those gushing funds.

The late Senator Paul Simon wrote in his memoir:

When I served in the Senate and got to my hotel room at midnight, there might be twenty phone calls waiting for me, nineteen from people whose names I did not recognize, the twentieth from someone who gave me a $1,000 campaign contribution or raised money for me. At midnight, I'm not going to make twenty phone calls. I might make one. Which one do you think I will make? So will every other incumbent Senator. That means that the financially articulate have inordinate access to policy matters. Access spells influence. The problem permeates our government and too often dictates what we do.[3]

Multiply Simon's thousand-dollar contribution by ten or a hundred, or even a thousand, and you can understand the cries that Washington is broken. During the last two years of their terms, if they're in competitive races, senators will devote well over half of their time to fund-raising. It involves hours and hours of "dialing for dollars," going to breakfasts, lunches, receptions, and dinners. It means hundreds of hours flying to cities all over the country for events. In my first and last campaigns for the Senate, for example, I flew to California more than thirty times.

Lobbyists generally preach to the choir, providing information and advice to activate already supportive senators to devote more time and effort to a particular bill or issue, rather than trying to win over lawmakers who oppose their cause. Even so, lobbyists do sometimes apply pressure, usually by deluging a senator's constituents with alarmist mailings, phone calls, and e-mails, urging them to tell the senator to vote a certain way on a given issue. Such "Astroturf" appeals, as opposed to genuine grass-roots outpourings, are generally easy to spot, and quickly discounted.

But some lobbying campaigns directly to the American people can spur powerful support. In the battle over the Clinton health care plan, both sides deployed extensive, orchestrated lobbying. As two top journalists wrote:

> Both sides quickly realized that traditional lobbying techniques—namely, cajoling congressmen and their aides behind closed doors—wouldn't work in this particular fight. President Clinton had taken the case to the American people; [Health Insurance Association of America] and [The National Federation of Independent Business] would do the same. . . . By the end of its campaign, HIAA had generated more than 45,000 phone calls, visits, and letters to Congress.[4]

HIAA's campaign featured the now-famous "Harry and Louise" television ads, in which a couple anguishes about what the plan will do to them. In all, opponents spent more than $100 million to defeat health care reform, while supporters spent only $15 million, the Center for Public Integrity estimated.

Efforts to regulate lobbying go back to the early twentieth century. In 1935, Hugo Black chaired a special Senate investigation of public utility company lobbyists, as Congress considered legislation to break up the giant "power trusts." An onslaught of telegrams hit senators' offices, protesting the probe. Suspecting that the utility lobbyists had orchestrated the protests, Black introduced a bill to require all lobbyists to register their names, salaries, expenses, and objectives with the secretary of the Senate. Black subpoenaed lobbyists, executives, and telegraph records, and proved that private citizens had paid for only three of the 15,000 protesting telegrams sent to Capitol Hill. The rest, Black said, were ginned up by a "high-powered, deceptive, telegram-fixing, letter-framing, Washington-visiting $5 million lobby." Black's investigation produced the first congressional system for registering lobbyists, and helped him win appointment to the Supreme Court.

We urgently need better balance between encouraging participation in the political and legislative process and limiting both the influence and the extraordinary amount of time dedicated today to fund-raising. If the Senate is Washington's "saucer" into which legislation is poured to cool, the saucer is cracked and may break clean through if not fixed soon. As an indication of how things have changed in fifty years, it is noteworthy that Robert Caro hardly mentions this problem in his books about LBJ.

29. THE COMMITTEE PROCESS

Nearly all legislation introduced in the Senate is referred to a committee. The committee, or sometimes a subcommittee that specializes in the particular issue area, may then hold hearings to explore the issues and assess remedies. Hearings provide senators a chance to gather information, express views, draw public attention to an issue, and apply pressure. The hearings are almost always open to the public, and sometimes televised, depending on news interest. The one exception is the Intelligence Committee, which deals with confidential material; many if not most of its hearings are closed.

A committee or subcommittee identifies and selects witnesses, generally aiming for diverse backgrounds and views. Committees may invite as many witnesses as they choose to a given hearing, and may hold that hearing over several days. Witnesses may come from federal, state, or local government; academia; interest groups; business; or may be private citizens. Committees sometimes invite celebrities to testify, especially those who have advocated for a cause, to generate attention. Only invited witnesses may testify. Senate rules allow a committee's minority-party members to call at least some witnesses, except on the Appropriations Committee. The Finance Committee allows every committee member to invite witnesses.

At hearings, witnesses generally make opening statements and then field committee members' questions. Beyond that, formats can vary widely: traditional, in which witnesses appear in the committee room before a dais of members; panel, in which a group of witnesses, generally including members with opposing viewpoints, appear together; joint, in which both House members and senators participate, to avoid holding similar hearings in both chambers; high-tech, in which witnesses testify remote through video link-ups; and field, in which one or more senators holds a hearing outside Washington, often in an area relevant to the subject. Field hearings have become increasingly popular. Generally, to qualify as an official hearing, members of both parties must attend.

Most witnesses jump at an invitation to testify before the Senate, which offers a chance to advance their views and raise their profiles. But for those less enthusiastic, the Senate has subpoena power, or the authority to compel testimony and delivery of documents and other materials. At the extreme, the Senate can charge reluctant witnesses with contempt of Congress, which carries a possible fine or prison term. The Senate has occasionally threatened to impeach officials who failed to produce information that committees requested.

After a committee finishes its research and investigation, often including hearings, it will "mark up," or edit, the bill. The committee's starting point is usually the "chairman's mark," or a draft of a bill as approved by the committee chairman. The committee may then rewrite much or all of the text, reflecting compromises and new ideas.

Sometimes turf wars break out between and among committees over a bill, each panel asserting or guarding its jurisdiction. Some committees use "border cops" to keep other committees from incurring on what they see as their turf. When a bill, or components of it, are assigned to more than one committee, competition can break out to get the bill done first, as with the Health, Education, Labor and Pensions (HELP) and Finance committees on the health care legislation under President Obama. In that case, the two committee chairmen had different strategies for advancing the measure. Finance Chairman Max Baucus (D-Mont.), looking for common ground, held off moving a bill until he had Republican cosponsors—a goal that he was never able to achieve. Chris Dodd (D-Conn.), filling in for ailing HELP chairman Ted Kennedy, was also looking for common ground, but chose to use the normal legislative process to do so. He scheduled a committee markup and considered over three hundred Republican amendments, at least a third of which were accepted. Dodd was also very inclusive of both administration and caucus leadership and therefore guided the bill through the mark-up process with Democratic priorities largely intact. In retrospect, Dodd's approach was better.

If a committee sends legislation to the full Senate, with or without amendments or recommendations, it must include a report outlining and justifying its changes and actions. Generally, a bill that ultimately passes the Senate still closely resembles the version "reported out" by the committee, a testament to the expert committee process.

Even so, the committee process and "regular order" are not always the cleanest or most efficient ways to legislate. The Majority

Leader may send legislation directly to the full Senate, bypassing committees, using one of several techniques, including appointing a task force to produce the legislation or simply placing the bill on the Calendar of General Orders. Evading regular order carries risks, though. In floor debate, a bill may draw divisive amendments that might have been worked out in committee markups. Opponents of special task forces interpret the leadership as saying, "We have this legislation we want to shove down your throat," as Ritchie put it.

Sometimes congressional leaders work out legislation among themselves, especially when facing ferocious time pressure, as on crafting an omnibus, or all-encompassing, appropriations bill to keep government operations funded. That's how we began handling legislation in the wake of the September 11 attacks, usually in the House Speaker's office, negotiating often late into the night. This approach requires extraordinary trust and cooperation.

As we turned to the White House's proposed economic stimulus package, the Speaker told me that we would now be using "regular order." The legislation would be drafted in the Senate Finance and House Ways and Means committees and then sent to the Senate and House floors for debate and amendment. When it was clear that the Bush tax cuts would not enjoy the same level of trust and cooperation as earlier legislative work in response to 9/11, the Speaker was acknowledging that "regular order" would be highly politicized and much more confrontational.

Differences came to a boil in mid-October, even though Democrats and Republicans agreed with Federal Reserve chairman Alan Greenspan's assessment that the government should step in with a combination of new spending and tax cuts. Democrats wanted to put the money into the hands of low- and middle-income workers, partly through unemployment benefits for those who had lost jobs, reasoning that those people needed the funds most and would spend them quickly, pumping the money back into the economy—which is the definition of a stimulus. Republicans wanted the bulk of the money directed toward tax cuts for businesses and individuals with higher incomes, to "kick-start" the economy from the top.

We knew that the economic stimulus was about to get politicized, and extended indefinitely as both sides postured. Immediately, the debate over how best to stimulate our economy put us back at one of those baseline differences that defined us. *Time* magazine ran a lead story, titled, "The End of Unity."

☆ 30. FLOOR ACTION ☆

On a typical day in the Senate, after the prayer and Pledge of Allegiance, the Majority Leader outlines the day's agenda. Often consulting with the Minority Leader, the Majority Leader schedules measures for votes, drawing from the Calendar of General Orders, which covers all legislation, and the Executive Calendar, which covers treaties and nominations.

Under the Senate's flexible scheduling system, nearly all bills are called up by unanimous consent. In every senator's office, a "Hotline" rings on designated staff telephones, carrying descriptions and deadlines for each bill. Senators are deemed in favor of a UC unless they formally object. Increasingly, unanimous consent has become harder to achieve. The majority of bills now require getting cloture on the motion to proceed, which is why some now call the Senate a 60-vote institution.

Unanimous consent measures advance through bipartisan trust, but can get snagged in differing interpretations or expectations. Oleszek cited "an especially contentious case" involving a major Republican priority:

Many Senators expected to vote on February 28, 1995, on final passage of a constitutional amendment to balance the budget . . . To the chagrin of opponents, Majority Leader Robert J. Dole, R-Kan., recessed the Senate because he was one vote short of the sixty-seven (or two-thirds) needed to pass a Constitutional amendment. "I thought a deal was a deal," complained Minority Leader Tom Daschle, D-S.D. . . . Dole was unable to find another vote, and the Senate defeated the centerpiece of the GOP's Contract with America.[1]

Dole's move was surprising—but he was well within the rules. Unanimous consent requests on legislation can sometimes serve largely partisan purposes, as Oleszek details in another example, on a UC on the 1999 Ed-Flex bill and my negotiations with Republican Leader Lott:

In the aftermath of President Clinton's impeachment trial and subsequent acquittal by the Senate, Majority Leader Trent Lott wanted to accelerate action on popular issues and refocus public attention on legislative accomplishments. Therefore, Lott called up a measure—waiving certain educational requirements and popularly referred to as "ed-flex"—that enjoyed broad bipartisan support . . . Democrats, however, wanted to showcase the differences between the parties on education especially with the 2000 elections as the backdrop, and offered various amendments advocated by President Clinton. . . . Majority Leader Daschle said to Lott, "Look. We will agree to these five or six amendments; and then let's move on." The last thing Lott wanted was to permit a high-profile debate on Democratic initiatives when Republicans hoped to claim education as one of their top priorities. . . . In the end, the two sides reached a unanimous consent agreement that served their respective purposes. Republicans achieved a final vote on the bill, and they defeated the Democratic amendments on party-line votes. . . . Democrats . . . won media coverage of their educational proposals and gained the opportunity to offer and debate a series of prized amendments.[2]

To avoid getting bogged down on one matter, perhaps over a contentious UC request, the Senate can dual- or even multitrack. But the approach has drawbacks and risks.

In August 2002, the Senate had to handle two key national legislative challenges, both requiring significant time, before they could end the session prior to the November elections: Creating the Department of Homeland Security and, following two major corporate scandals, reforming pension systems to protect retirees. Senators also had to tackle many of the remaining appropriations bills that must be passed each year by October 1 to fund various federal departments and agencies.

To meet this schedule, we began dual-tracking, moving during the workday between the two pieces of legislation. But it immediately became clear that Republicans didn't share the Democrats' sense of urgency. As soon as the bills reached the Senate floor, Republicans filibustered them. And as soon as the filibusters began, we had to set everything aside to deal with a new issue—a resolution to give the president war-making powers to deal with the threats posed by Iraq.

For most bills that come to the floor, each Leader has to pick a manager, to work speaking rosters and lineups. Usually, the leader designates the committee chairman as manager, but not always.

Sometimes the committee chair isn't as conversant on the subject and you pick an expert within the caucus. Or sometimes two or three committees have joint jurisdiction over a bill, and you have to pick one of those committee chairmen.

The health bill during the Obama administration offers a good example. Drafts went through the Health, Education, Labor and Pensions Committee and the Finance Committee, and Majority Leader Harry Reid had those two committee chairmen share the responsibility for managing the bill on the Senate floor, depending on the title, or component.

Debate in the modern Senate generally features shorter speeches than in the nineteenth century, when the Great Triumvirate—Webster, Clay, and Calhoun—held forth with hours of stirring oratory. Today's hectic pace and crammed calendar do not afford such luxury. But today's Senate speeches have generally improved over those before the Cable-Satellite Public Affairs Network (C-SPAN) began televising the Senate in June 1986. C-SPAN's arrival was gradual, reaching the Senate floor only after its cameras became fixtures at committee hearings, news briefings, and other congressional events.

C-SPAN is a critical tool to openness and to transparency, but also carries some downsides. Senators, just by the nature of politics, oftentimes speak to the cameras more than to their colleagues. They're more guarded about what they say in front of a camera than behind one. And, unfortunately, the cameras have constrained some of the honesty and candor that is so important to good legislating. They've also had a profound effect on floor attendance; if you can watch all the action from your office, why go to the floor? Why not stay in your office and do two things at once? Oftentimes, members do.

Still, once in a while, for a highly classified debate at which the Senate will discuss top-secret material, officers close the galleries and senators abandon their current chamber with all its electronic equipment for the Old Chamber. There, they can discuss the most modern, technology-driven secrets in the Capitol's oldest space, which also connects them to the past.

Recently, I was roundly rebuked by an audience when I suggested that today's Senate is the most transparent in history. Because of its transparency, the Senate's internal workings—both good and bad—are more exposed than ever. Ironically, that exposure has created greater skepticism among many Americans about the legislative process than they had prior to the introduction of C-SPAN.

☆ 31. AMENDMENTS ☆

Any senator, at least in theory, may offer any amendment to any bill—a hallmark of the Senate. On the floor, senators may offer amendments to bills, called first-degree amendments, or to other amendments, called second-degree amendments. Senate rules do not allow third-degree amendments. Amendments may take several forms, either to strike text, insert text, or strike and insert. Amendments also vary in scope, from a substitute, which replaces a bill's entire text; to perfecting, which inserts or replaces some of the text. Rules govern each type of amendment as to precedence, or priority, and time. And those rules must be considered when devising legislative strategy and tactics.

As an example, let's go back to the Patriot Act, and Attorney General Ashcroft's demand that Congress pass the proposals within days. My alternative, which ultimately passed with bipartisan support, was technically a substitute to Ashcroft's legislation.

I also pressed perfecting amendments to legislation in the wake of the September 11 attacks. Faced with experts' warnings that some commercial airlines were on the verge of collapse, threatening the entire industry, the Senate considered legislation to stabilize the sector. Initially, the proposal was simple: $5 billion in direct aid for losses stemming from September 11, and $10 billion in loan guarantees. While the proposal called for the federal government to bail out an airline industry with billions of dollars, it provided nothing for its 150,000 workers, who had lost their jobs in the month following September 11. Democrats were sympathetic to the thousands of airline workers who were out of work as a result of the crisis.

Senator Jean Carnahan (D-Mo.) and I crafted an amendment to the bill that would guarantee those workers health care and unemployment insurance. We were simply attempting to achieve parity. On the Senate floor, we tried to persuade Republicans to help the economic victims of 9/11. Republicans filibustered our amendment, and we came up four votes short of the sixty needed for cloture.

In practice, senators often face procedural limitations on their right to offer any amendment to any bill—which have been used increasingly to shut out the minority party.

At the extreme, the Majority Leader can exploit his right of first recognition to "fill the amendment tree," precluding any other senator from offering an amendment. Technically, a senator loses the floor once he or she files an amendment, but the Majority Leader can exercise his right of first recognition to file one amendment and then immediately seek recognition to file another, both first and second degree, until no more amendments may be hung on the "tree" under the agreed-upon rules. The idea is to prevent opponents from forcing votes on proposals that would either embarrass the majority or change the bill. Filling the amendment tree shuts out the minority, forcing its members to vote on legisla-

tion without a chance to debate or shape it, often prompting retaliation through the minority's best and sometimes only recourse,
filibusters. That, in turn, brings gridlock.

Both Republican and Democrat leaders have filled the tree.
As Leader, I *rarely* filled the tree. In a year, I may have filled it
once or twice. It should be a last resort; something you really
don't want to do. The tactic creates very serious relationship issues
with the minority party. The effect, regardless of who's doing it, is
exactly the same—it alienates and frustrates and exacerbates the
problem.

32. THE YEAS AND NAYS

☆ ☆

For matters not decided by unanimous consent, formal Senate votes can deliver drama and intrigue—even before the clerk calls a single senator's name. Roll call votes offer an occasion for senators to gather and talk on the floor or in the cloakrooms. Senators often arrange to meet during votes, and seasoned journalists watch from the balcony to see who's talking to whom, read the body language, develop theories, and pursue stories. An astute observer who knows that one senator is seeking support for a controversial bill and sees him put an arm around another senator's shoulder—a Senate sign for a private conversation—may be on the way to a scoop.

Senators cast votes in one of three ways: by voice; by division, when senators stand for a rough count; and by roll call, the famous yeas and nays. Rules on voting, like most other Senate rules, are complex and arcane. Any senator who has the floor may "ask for the yeas and nays" on a pending matter, and senators often do so immediately after introducing an amendment. Yeas and nays are granted only if a senator draws one fifth of a quorum who agree to the motion. But even if approved, the roll call vote will not occur until the debate has ended, sometimes hours or days later—or never.

When roll call votes are called, according to rules determined for each Congress, senators have a certain time period in which to vote, generally fifteen minutes. In recent years, the fifteen-minute rule has evolved into something much longer. It is not uncommon to keep a vote open for over an hour to accommodate a missing senator. Stacked votes, taken in a series, come at closer intervals. But the Majority Leader has ways to stretch a vote's time, if he's inclined, if a senator is running late, or if the majority is working to sway some undecided or opposed colleagues. When the presiding officer calls a vote, bells and lights go off throughout the Senate complex, summoning members.

Senators are expected to vote on every roll call, and the media and interest groups keep tabs. Some groups issue scorecards and ratings based on a basket of key votes. But the Senate makes some provisions for missing a vote, such as pairing. By pairing, two senators who disagree on a measure strike an arrangement to offset their votes on a roll call, generally when one of them has to be absent. Neither of them votes, but the pairing is recorded. Paired votes also count toward a quorum.

With a closely divided Senate, key votes often come down to a single senator. One episode, in particular, has entered Senate lore, when Republicans needed Pete Wilson, a California Republican who had been hospitalized, for a 1985 deficit package vote. Bob Dole recounted the episode as well as I've heard it told:

> In counting heads, it looked like we were headed for a tie vote: 49 Republicans plus one courageous Democrat, the late Ed Zorinsky of Nebraska. The plan was for the tie to be broken by then-Vice President Bush. And then, suddenly,

Pete Wilson was taken to Bethesda for an emergency appendectomy. He said later he wished it was a lobotomy.

I called his doctors and asked if Pete could physically withstand a trip to Capitol Hill. How long could he stay? Would he have to be sedated? It occurred to me, in any event. . . . Well, the doctors recommended he not make the trip. But Pete had other ideas. I also promised him good press coverage. That will get any senator out of bed, I think.

I will never forget the sound of the ambulance sirens at 2 in the morning, or the sight of Pete in his pajamas and a robe, sitting in a wheelchair and hooked up to an IV, being rolled into the Senate Chamber to a standing ovation from both sides of the aisle.[1]

33. "THE THIRD HOUSE OF CONGRESS"

Before legislation can go to the president for signature and become law, it must pass the House and Senate in identical form. Sometimes differences between the versions of a measure passed by each chamber can be striking. To resolve these differences, one chamber can pass the other chamber's bill; the two chambers can "ping-pong" amendments back and forth until the bills become identical; or the House and Senate can go to conference, in which representatives of each chamber meet to produce a unified measure. Those "conference reports" then go for up-or-down votes in each chamber, with no opportunity to amend. If a conference report passes, it goes to the president for signature. If it fails, the bill is usually dead.

The conference process does not guarantee that the final bill will represent a neat compromise between the House and Senate versions. Conferees may "violate scope," striking provisions—including those that had been in both bills—and adding new measures. No statistics are kept, but the incidence seems to be increasing. A few years ago, without hearings or debate in either chamber, a $50 billion tobacco industry tax break was quietly inserted, in one forty-six-word sentence, into a budget conference report, which the president then signed into law. When word leaked about the tax break, it was repealed in another law.[1] On rare occasions, party leaders revise a conference report, adding or deleting material, which can spark anger. Anticipating a conference, the House or Senate will sometimes strategically add or withhold measures, saving those issues as bargaining chips in conference.

Conferences are sometimes called "the third house" of Congress, in which a small number of selected members shape a final bill. When I arrived in the Senate, conferences were used on nearly all legislation. By the time I became Leader, it was still well over 50 percent of the time. Now, conferences are used only occasionally, on about 10 percent of passed legislation.

Conferences aren't extinct, but they're on the endangered species list. That's unfortunate, because more and more now, staffs negotiate differences between a bill's two versions. Conversations are held on the telephone. Chairmen and leaders of House and Senate committees of jurisdiction talk between and among themselves, and then, ultimately, things are decided almost as a fait accompli.

That's not the way good legislation should be written. There should be transparency and openness, which a conference facilitates. An ad hoc committee should work through the differences, hold a good debate, resolve issues one by one, and then bring its conference report back to the House and Senate.

The conference process formally begins when one chamber requests a conference and the other agrees. Then the party leaders select their conferees, and sometimes instruct them. Sometimes party leaders hammer out an agreement and dictate it to the conferees, which can largely defeat the purpose. Sometimes the leaders actually serve as conferees, especially on high-stakes legislation.

Senate Republican Leader Bill Frist and I both served as conferees on a measure to provide prescription drug benefits through Medicare, a major expansion that had set off a fiery debate. House Ways and Means Chairman Bill Thomas, a California Republican, was chair of the conference because the GOP controlled the House. Thomas grew so angry at me that he literally locked me out of the conference, which was unprecedented. I arrived at the newly refurbished room in the basement of the Capitol where conferees were meeting, and the door was locked. I could have had the sergeant at arms require Thomas to open it. But I chose not to do that. Eventually, we reconvened. But Thomas's move shows how contentious things can get.

Sometimes two versions of a bill seem absolutely irreconcilable, with or without a conference. For example, for years, House Republicans and Senate Democrats could not come together on funding the Federal Aviation Administration, an agency within the Department of Transportation that oversees and regulates all private and commercial air travel, leading to twenty-three separate temporary extensions of the FAA bill that passed in 2006. A partial shutdown of the agency for two weeks during the summer of 2011 caused furloughs of four thousand FAA staff and cost the government an estimated $400 million in uncollected airline ticket taxes.

In August 2011, the congressional effort collapsed over standards for recognizing a labor union. House Republicans insisted on a standard of majority support from all union members, not just a majority of those who voted in an election about unionizing—which would be like requiring a Senate candidate to win a majority of all the registered voters in a state. Nobody would ever win, because you'd never get a majority.

The National Labor Relations Board passed a rule setting the standard as a majority of those who vote. House Republicans grew furious, and took away essential air service funding for thirteen communities, primarily in Nevada and West Virginia, home states of the two leading Senate Democrats on the issue, Harry Reid and Jay Rockefeller. The move was a significant change in approach, and escalation. Finally, in February 2012, Congress passed a compromise bill to fund the FAA through 2015. But the situation makes a good illustration of the chaos that occurs when Congress breaks down.

34. VETOES AND OVERRIDES

When Congress does send a bill or joint resolution passed by both chambers to the president, the Constitution requires the chief executive to take one of several actions, or no action. The president may sign the measure into law within ten days when Congress remains in session; veto it, returning the bill to the chamber that sent it, along with a veto message stating his objections; take no action, which makes the bill a law after ten days; or issue a "pocket veto" by not signing the legislation when Congress has adjourned.

When the House or Senate receives a vetoed piece of legislation, the Constitution requires that chamber to "reconsider" it, which generally means referring the bill back to committee; or voting on overriding the president's veto, either immediately or at a later scheduled time.

To override a veto, both the House and Senate must vote by two-thirds majority to make the bill into a law over the president's objections. That's a high hurdle. As we've seen, it's difficult to build a majority coalition in the Senate on controversial legislation, tougher to muster sixty votes, or three fifths, to end a filibuster; and daunting to gather two thirds of all senators. And that's without overruling the president. In our nation's history, Congress has overridden barely one hundred presidential vetoes. Given the odds, senators should consider the prospect of a veto in crafting legislation. The president's threat of a veto is often enough to halt or reshape a bill.

In recent decades, one of the most dramatic override efforts came in 1987 over President Reagan's veto of an $87.5 billion highway bill. As Bob Dole recounted, his job as Majority Leader was to sustain the veto, and Republicans at first thought they had prevailed by a single vote. Then Robert Byrd convinced a North Carolina Democrat to change his vote and support an override, and Dole was unable to convince any of the thirteen Republicans who had voted to override to change theirs. Dole recalled:

At this point, President Reagan said he wished to meet with the Republican Senators. Not wanting to see the President embarrassed by what I believed was a losing effort, I advised against him coming to the Hill. He came anyway to make his case in person. I can still see him pleading with [Idaho Republican] Steve Symms . . . almost begging him.

In the end, our one-vote majority turned into a one-vote loss. Yet, while we may have lost on the highway bill, the bigger loss would have been to do nothing. As any true leader, President Reagan knew that success is never final nor defeat fatal as long as you have the courage to act on principle."[1]

The timing of sending and signing bills can have significant political effect. In July 2001, Congress was working on a supplemental appropriations bill for the military, to provide funds to cover unanticipated operations and other expenses. Vice President Dick Cheney phoned me, urging the Senate to pass the final bill that day. Without immediate Senate action, Cheney told me, military pay raises would be deferred and some training exercises would be canceled. I had already announced that the Senate would hold no further roll call votes that day, a Friday. I quickly phoned a number of senators and pressed them to allow us to pass the bill by unanimous consent, which we were able to do later that day. Given the urgency the vice president had stressed, I expected President Bush to sign the bill as soon as it reached the White House. Instead, the president waited four days and took the bill with him to Kosovo, where he signed it in front of a legion of cheering troops, saying, "I promised America that help is on the way for the men and women who wear our uniform." No training exercises were canceled, that I know of.[2]

PART
4

BUDGETS,
INVESTIGATIONS,
SPECIAL SENATE
FUNCTIONS

★ ★ ★　　★ ★ ★

35. THE FEDERAL BUDGET PROCESS

☆

The federal budget—like any government budget, even that of a small town—is more than a table of dollars and cents; it's a political document laying out priorities and values. How much of your limited funds do you want to spend building or fixing highways, preserving national parks, combatting terrorism, or investing in research to cure cancer? Or on the gamut of other needs, all competing for pieces of the federal pie? The process of dividing and doling out funds sparks passionate, partisan debate, and draws advocates for every cause seeking a line on the ledger.

As to the legislative mechanics, the federal budget process has perplexed—and frustrated—generations of policymakers. The "budget reform" of the 1970s, Congress's latest effort to put budget discipline into practice, has been a complete failure.

The Constitution gives Congress the power of the purse; sole authority to collect taxes, to borrow money, to authorize expenditures—in short, to provide the funds that keep the country running and secure. The administration may spend only those funds Congress has approved, as specified. An adage holds, "The President proposes, Congress disposes."

The Constitution dictates that spending bills must begin in the House, but does not spell out the budget process, a complex and evolving procedure that the Senate and House handle according to their own rules.

In 1921, Congress tasked the president with submitting an annual federal budget, essentially a proposal to Congress. Theoretically, the president submits a detailed budget request by the first Monday in February. Lawmakers review the president's proposal, hold hearings, act on mandatory items and craft a blueprint, a concurrent resolution known as a "budget resolution" for spending it expects to approve, targets for revenue, and multiyear priorities. (Remember, a concurrent resolution must be approved by both chambers of Congress, but does not go to the president for signature, and so does not carry the force of law.)

To prevent filibusters on budget bills, the Senate limits debate on the budget resolution to fifty hours. In addition, to handle the avalanche of amendments that usually pours in, the Senate votes on one amendment after another, usually well into the night, sessions informally called "votoramas."

In practice, deadlines set in the 1970s reform have not been met for a long time. With a budget resolution in place—in theory by April 15, though Congress has not met that deadline in many years—Congress then authorizes and appropriates funds, in two separate and distinct steps (much more on that shortly) and later oversees and audits the executive branch's spending of those funds.

Two thirds of the budget goes to "direct" spending, set by previously enacted law for paying interest on the national debt; pensions and benefits; defense; and mandatory programs, called entitlements, including Social Security and Medicare. "Discretionary" spending, the remaining one third of the budget, covers the gamut from highway projects to the Commission on Fine Arts, and falls more easily under budget crafters' control. Congress can also adjust direct spending, but it takes a change in the authorization; that is, a change in the law that sets government obligations and authorizes automatic funding. Budget negotiators often spend months trying to find the right combination of changes in entitlements, mandatory spending, and discretionary accounts.

For decades, Congress called entitlement programs, particularly Social Security and Medicare, "the third rail" of federal spending—touch it and you perish politically, a play on urban subway systems. Funding for these programs was deliberately kept separate, in so-called "lockboxes," to prevent officials from depleting it for general expenses.

Congress also handles a small portion of federal spending off the books, the so-called black budgets, for secret military-related projects. But even those budgets are not immune to politics. Howard Baker told a story about his Senate predecessor from Tennessee, Kenneth McKellar, who in 1939 chaired the Appropriations Committee. When President Roosevelt summoned McKellar to the White House to ask him whether he could hide a billion dollars for Roosevelt's ultra-top-secret national defense project, McKellar replied, "Well, Mr. President, of course I can—and where in Tennessee are we going to build this plant?"[1]

Congress's annual appropriations bills are due for the president's signature by October 1, the beginning of the government's fiscal year. But Congress often misses deadlines on its established budget schedule. Instead of moving a dozen separate bills to cover the various federal departments, Congress sometimes produces "omnibus" budget bills, which its leaders craft in the frenzied final weeks and days late in the fiscal or calendar year. Omnibus bills are huge legislative packages that bundle a host of initiatives covering various agencies, forcing enormous compromises, and inflaming friction between Congress and the president.

For many of the years during the past decade, Congress produced no budget at all. When lawmakers realize they won't meet their October 1 deadline, they pass—or try to pass—a continuing resolution, or CR, which maintains spending at the current year's levels, literally buying some time to hammer out an agreement. Congress may pass a series of CRs, some lasting months, some lasting only a few days, each time hoping to reach resolution on that year's budget, too often eventually resigning themselves to reaching no agreement. Impasses on budget bills led to federal government shutdowns in 1995 and 1996, after President Clinton vetoed appropriations bills and Congress refused to pass a CR, and nearly again in 2011.

The shutdown that began in mid-December 1995 hit at a very wintery time, and congressional leaders needed four-wheel drive vehicles to get through the snow to reach the White House, where we gathered with President Clinton to negotiate a resolution to the impasse.

Once we arrived, it was hard to leave because of the weather, and so we just settled in, of all places, in the Oval Office. It was President Clinton, Vice President Al Gore, Clinton Chief of Staff Leon Panetta, Bob Dole, House Speaker Newt Gingrich (R-Ga.), House Minority Leader Dick Gephardt (D-Mo.), and me. We sat there for hours and hours. Days turned to nights and we kept sitting there, with a whiteboard in front of us.

Back then, Gingrich, just as he is now, was somewhat volatile, and a couple of times he got very angry and stomped out. One of the times he stomped out, it was at night and Dole kind of shrugged and looked at us and followed him out.

Because of the weather, Gingrich probably wasn't going to go anywhere. Most likely, he was going to come back. So the president said, "How about if we just watch a movie?"

So he put a film into a VCR in a room just off the Oval Office, popped some microwave popcorn, and we watched a movie.

Some days later, we were nearing the end of our negotiations, and now it was really bumping up against Christmas, and Gingrich and I were having lunch. We were talking about Christmas, and I just assumed that we were going to have to be at the White House the day before and the day after the holiday, and into the week between Christmas and New Year's. So Newt and I were sharing stories about what our plans *had* been.

I said, "Well, my parents were celebrating their fiftieth wedding anniversary, so for the first time ever we had gotten them a cruise for three or four days down in the Caribbean; we were going to go with them." I said the rest of my family was going to go, and I'd just have to stay.

And he said, "Oh, that's too bad; you shouldn't have to do that."

I said, "Well, I don't know how else to get around it."

After the lunch, we went back into our meeting and Gingrich announced, "I have a suggestion." He said, "You know, we've made a lot of decisions here that really need to be scored, just to see if we're close to where we think we are." That is, he was saying we needed neutral government experts to analyze the dollar-and-cents effects of our plans. "I would propose that we take a four- or five-day break." And then Newt looked at me and winked.

And that's what we did. So I got to go on my cruise with my parents as they celebrated their fiftieth wedding anniversary.

Beyond the annual appropriations bills, Congress often passes supplemental appropriations bills, or "supplementals," to cover unexpected emergencies, such as for disaster relief or war. Those urgent bills offer opportunities to add funding for unrelated pet projects, often spurring calls to pass a "clean" CR.

To better manage the process, Congress in 1921 created what is now the Office of Management and Budget within the executive branch, which develops the president's budget request, among other duties; and in 1974 created the Congressional Budget Office, which provides lawmakers with objective, nonpartisan analyses of the president's budget proposals, and Senate and House Budget Committees. But the budget process still needs much improvement.

In recent decades, the federal government has usually spent more in a given year than it has taken in, producing annual deficits that require the federal government to borrow funds to make up the difference, adding to a growing national debt. Deficits are like extra weight, some say; easy to put on, but hard to take off. But recently, as the federal debt has reached crisis levels, many lawmakers and other leaders have recognized the need to cut sacred programs and raise additional tax revenue—though they continue to mire on specifics.

In early 2010, President Obama created the National Commission on Fiscal Responsibility and Reform, better known as Bowles-Simpson or Simpson-Bowles after cochairs Alan Simpson and Erskine Bowles, to put us on track toward long-term "fiscal sustainability." The commission issued a report, but failed to win the required supermajority support from its members to endorse its plan.

In mid-2011, the federal government was running out of money and heading for default on its debts, for the first time in history, as an August 2 deadline approached for raising the country's self-imposed debt limit, then $14.3 trillion, and all sides continued to spar. The debt limit, the total amount of money the government is authorized to borrow to meet its obligations, was created in the twentieth century, initially during World War I as part of a package to allow greater spending flexibility, with revisions shortly before World War II. It's really unnecessary, and had routinely been raised dozens of times. But not in 2011.

Some members of Congress, including one major candidate for the 2012 Republican presidential nomination, brushed off a default, calling it less problematic than failing to tame federal spending. In the final weeks and days before deadline, meetings collapsed and the president and congressional leaders held angry news conferences and blamed the other side. The chairman of the Federal Reserve and the president of the U.S. Chamber of Commerce warned that a failure to act could trigger a financial meltdown.[2] Financial markets swooned and the world drew a lasting perception of Washington dysfunction.

After intense negotiations to nearly the last minute, leaders came up with a compromise that would, as President Obama described it, "allow us to avoid default and end the crisis that Washington imposed on the rest of America." The compromise raised the debt ceiling by $2.4 trillion, required steep spending cuts, and created a joint, bipartisan Congressional committee to find most of those cuts. If the "supercommittee," as it soon became known, failed to agree on specific cuts by a November 23 deadline, $1.2 trillion in automatic cuts would trigger, half from defense.

Despite the agreement, much lasting damage had already been done. In early August, one of the major rating agencies, Standard & Poor's, downgraded the United States, stripping our vaunted AAA status. As CNN reported, "S&P also cited dysfunctional policymaking in Washington as a factor in the downgrade. 'The political brinksmanship of recent months highlights what we see as America's governance and policymaking becoming less stable, less effective, and less predictable than what we previously believed.'"[3]

In November 2011, days before its deadline, the super committee formally announced failure.

36. AUTHORIZING AND APPROPRIATING

In approving federal spending, Congress takes two separate, sequential steps: It authorizes spending to create or continue an agency or program, and then it appropriates funds to carry out those authorizations. The two-step process is designed to bring greater accountability and effectiveness in dispensing federal treasure. Separate committees and subcommittees handle each step of the process.

In the Senate, standing committees, such as the Committee on Environment and Public Works, authorize legislation covering the agencies and programs they oversee. An authorizing measure may also spell out an agency's or a program's duties, functions, organizational structure, and its officials' responsibilities. The measure may specify the amount to be spent, or may provide "such sums as may be necessary." Authorizers, especially, shape policy.

The Appropriations Committee, initially through its dozen subcommittees, then reviews the various authorizations and sets aside funds—or doesn't—to cover them. Each Appropriations subcommittee oversees specific areas of federal spending and produces its own bill. Because of their sweeping authority and clout, those subcommittee chairmen are sometimes called the College of Cardinals.

Technically, an appropriations measure provides budget authority to allow federal agencies to incur obligations and authorizes payments from the Treasury. By standing rules, senators may not legislate on appropriations bills, though there are various ways around that.

Even so, the congressional budget process carries an inherent conflict between authorizers and appropriators . . . and sometimes conflicts of interest, or at least limited checks, as some senators play roles in both steps of the process. At this writing, one senator chairs both the HELP Committee, which authorizes spending, and the Appropriations subcommittee on Labor, Health and Human Services and Education, which appropriates funds for those authorizations.

Senate subcommittees and committees dissect the president's budget request as they would any proposal. They hold hearings, allowing the stakeholders—in this case, the administration and its agencies—to plead their cases. Since all money bills have to originate in the House, Senate appropriations subcommittees wait for the House to send over draft bills, which they then amend. Senators work out any differences in markup sessions, and draft their parts of the budget resolution. Then the House and Senate work out inevitable differences between their two versions, often in conference.

What happens if the authorizers and appropriators all work their various pieces of the budget pie, and the numbers don't add up to the bottom line in the budget resolution? Then Congress performs a procedure called Reconciliation. Reconciliation, established in the Budget Act of 1974, allows Senate and House budget committees to order other committees within their respective bodies to reconcile their spending figures with the resolution; that is, to change existing law to adjust taxes, entitlements, other direct spending, or the federal debt limit. If the Senate Budget Committee issues a "reconciliation instruction" to only one committee, that committee reports a reconciliation bill. If the Senate Budget Committee instructs more than one committee, the Budget Committee will report an omnibus reconciliation bill. Debate on reconciliation is limited to twenty hours, also preventing filibusters.

Again, though, this is theoretical. Rarely does the Congress actually do it this way. Reconciliation bills are generally used now as vehicles for unrelated legislation in addition to the budget. But often nothing gets passed.

37. LEGISLATIVE ☆ OVERSIGHT AND ☆ INVESTIGATIONS

One of the Senate's primary functions is oversight of the executive branch.

"The ability of the Senate to discover relevant information, despite executive resistance, is an essential check on executive power," former vice president and senator Walter Mondale said. "It should be seen as one of the indispensable elements of the Senate's vitality and one of the basic reasons that America is the most powerful democratic country in the world."[1]

The Senate monitors the executive branch as it executes the laws and mandates Congress has passed, and holds agencies and the administration accountable. The process, largely public, exposes misfeasance, nonfeasance, and malfeasance, and produces laws to correct the problems, safeguarding the system. The appropriations process also serves as an oversight vehicle, in which senators can add to, reduce, or even zero-out funds, boosting or eliminating programs or agencies.

The Senate's main oversight tool is investigations, often formal and lengthy. In the 1920s, the Supreme Court confirmed congressional committees' right to probe any matter affecting existing laws, not just pending laws, and to subpoena witnesses and materials.

The Senate and congressional oversight role doesn't necessarily have to involve a contentious matter; the Senate performs a vital function by investigating anything problematic, in an effort to better explain to the American people why something is they way it is. It's really Congress's responsibility, constitutionally, to help explain to the American people why government is functioning as it is and why certain circumstances are as they are. Over time, I called for a host of investigations on matters ranging from increases in gas prices to problems associated with the economy to foreign crises.

Senators occasionally abuse the investigative role, even half a century after Senator Joseph McCarthy's notorious and shameful investigations into the threat of Communist subversion and spying. As chairman of the Senate Permanent Committee on Investigations in the early 1950s, McCarthy ran witch hunts to expose those he suspected of harboring communist sympathies. He bullied his targets, trampled civil rights, and destroyed careers on unfounded—or unproven—charges.

McCarthy's run ended when his own committee investigated a clash between the Wisconsin Republican and the U.S. Army. At the 1954 Army–McCarthy hearings, Army attorney Joseph Welch famously pleaded to McCarthy, "Have you no sense of decency, sir, at long last?" The Senate, by large bipartisan majority, censured McCarthy for conduct unbecoming a senator. Even today, an accusation of "McCarthyism," especially against a Senate investigation, is a heavy charge.

Today's missteps more often involve using investigations for political purposes. To guard against such abuses, senators have to be circumspect, and concerned about the degree to which a probe serves a constitutional role. A good example is the lead-up to the impeachment of President Clinton, when a special prosecutor spent enormous time, effort, and money, including public hearings, investigating the president's decades-old Whitewater real estate investment, all of which ultimately found insufficient evidence of any wrongdoing by the president or the First Lady. Then the special prosecutor, after announcing he was closing his probe, turned to new, unrelated tips about President Clinton, as we've discussed.

In part because of dispersed authority, congressional investigations can also be duplicative between the House and Senate, and sometimes within either body. After the 1996 elections, Republican chairmen of both the Senate and House Governmental Affairs Committees launched wide-ranging investigations into alleged financial abuses by President Clinton's successful reelection campaign, spending millions of dollars and ultimately drawing widespread rebuke, including an April 1997 *New York Times* editorial headlined, "A House Investigation Travesty."

The costs of Senate investigations extend beyond those of the committees in charge. It's amazing the amount of time anybody in the executive branch has to spend preparing for and testifying in front of the committees that are investigating a matter. At some point, this growing problem of duplication and inefficiency in congressional information gathering needs to be addressed.

But institutions, in many respects, are no better than the people who run them—in the Senate, as anywhere else. They work well when you've got dedicated professionals who strike good balances, and they work terribly when you don't. Any one of the Senate's institutional tools—investigations and filibusters among them—can be abused and undermined if people who are not appropriately motivated to do the right thing abuse their power and their responsibilities. That happens, unfortunately, more often than it should.

In the right hands, and in the right spirit, Senate investigations can—and have—checked power and safeguarded our institutions and our democracy.

In April 1922, the *Wall Street Journal* reported a secret deal in which Secretary of the Interior Albert Fall had leased the U.S. naval petroleum reserve at Teapot Dome, Wyoming, to a private oil company at low rates without competitive bidding. The Senate Committee on Public Lands investigated. Republicans expected the probe to prove futile, and let the committee's most junior Democrat, Thomas Walsh of Montana, take charge. Walsh eventually uncovered Fall's corrupted scheme not only at Teapot Dome, but also at Elk Hills, California. It was arguably the biggest government scandal to that point, and Walsh ultimately became a national hero while Fall went to prison.

Senate investigations often use public hearings, which can provide high drama. Hearings have produced indelible images and phrases, changed public consciousness, launched and destroyed careers, and inspired action.

When Harry Truman arrived in the Senate in 1935 as a product of Kansas City's Pendergast political machine, he was widely written off as a political hack. In 1940, the United States was preparing for entry into what was then a raging European conflict—and would soon become World War II—by appropriating $10 billion for defense contracts. Early in 1941, Truman learned of contractors' widespread mismanagement. He made a 10,000-mile tour of military bases and found waste and corruption in contracting that were hampering national mobilization. Truman proposed creating a Senate Committee to Investigate the National Defense Program, which the Senate eventually approved. For three years under Truman's chairmanship, the committee held hundreds of hearings and saved billions of dollars in waste and fraud. Truman emerged a star, admired and respected. In 1944, Franklin Roosevelt named Truman as his running mate in FDR's successful campaign for a fourth term. A year later, Truman would be president.

From 1950 to 1951, as Americans watched through a new device called television, Senator Estes Kefauver held hearings as part of an investigation into organized crime. The star witness, mob boss Frank Costello, asked the committee that he not be televised, and the committee asked the television networks to honor Costello's request. The networks showed Costello's hands, rather than his face. But images of the mobster's hands wringing under tough questioning told as much as any facial expression could have.

The Army–McCarthy hearings followed a few years later, and Watergate twenty years after that. Joseph Welch's cry about McCarthy's lack of decency still resonates today, while Howard Baker's rhetorical question at a Watergate hearing, "What did the President know, and when did he know it?" still often echoes, mostly in cases of alleged government cover-ups.

Perhaps the most famous congressional investigation looked into a burglary at Democratic National Committee headquarters at the Watergate complex during the 1972 presidential election and an alleged administration cover-up. As a rapt nation watched on television, a Senate investigatory committee, chaired by North Carolina Democrat Sam Ervin, found substantial evidence by questioning witnesses at public hearings. They found that the Nixon administration used "dirty tricks" against political opponents and that President Nixon had secretly tape-recorded Oval Office conversations. Nixon tried to withhold the tapes, claiming executive privilege, but the Supreme Court rejected his argument. Facing almost certain impeachment by the House and conviction by the Senate, Nixon resigned in August 1974.

In modern times, other seismic Senate hearings include the

1987 Iran-Contra hearings into a complex multinational web of illicit arms sales to Iran, funding for Nicaraguan rebels, and efforts to free American hostages, which nearly toppled Reagan's presidency; and Professor Anita Hill's testimony during Justice Clarence Thomas's 1991 confirmation hearings, which awakened America to sexual harassment and led to a wave of women in the Senate, which had been 98 percent male.

38. NOMINATIONS — ADVICE AND CONSENT

Under the Constitution, the president nominates high-ranking officials, including Cabinet secretaries, federal judges, ambassadors, and heads of agencies, boards, and commissions, and the Senate either confirms or rejects those nominees. The Advice and Consent clause leaves a lot of room for debate as to how much power the Senate can exercise in "advising" on the president's nominees; the Framers had varying views, and so have senators and presidents ever since.

In August 1789, the Senate for the first time rejected a presidential nominee, George Washington's choice for naval officer for the Port of Savannah, Georgia. Washington had not consulted with Georgia's two senators before making the nomination, and one of the senators preferred a close political ally for the post. Invoking the nascent custom of "senatorial courtesy," the Georgia senator rallied a majority of the Senate to reject Washington's man.

Senators still exercise great influence over who gets nominated and confirmed for positions within their states. Until the

1930s, a senator could quash a nomination for a federal position in his state simply by declaring the nominee "personally obnoxious."

Presidents began consulting with the Senate before making nominations, and sometimes compromised, bypassing their first choices in favor of nominees more likely to win confirmation. Enshrining senatorial courtesy, the Judiciary Committee in 1913 began the practice of "blue sheets," essentially refusing to advance a nomination out of committee unless both home-state senators signed a blue sheet of paper signifying approval. Presidents wound up choosing judicial nominees, especially for district courts, from lists that senators submitted. Some senators have even formed judicial nominating commissions within their states. But recently, as judicial nominations foundered in partisan gridlock, blue slips lost much of their clout.

Many nominees for judgeships and other federal positions go through Senate confirmation hearings, which can run days or even weeks, after months of preparation on both sides. The hearings get nominees on record about their policy views, on which they can later be held accountable. Senators often express anger and frustration when federal judges, who get lifetime appointments, veer from their stated positions once they're seated, a shift derided as "confirmation conversion."

In the Senate, many nominations tap deep-seated feelings about both issues and personalities, and you get caught up in lot of these debates. The inclination, oftentimes, is to use all the rules and tools available to you if you feel passionately about a particular nomination—either to pass it or to stop it. Stopping a nomination is increasingly done through the minority's most valuable asset, the filibuster.

We considered filibustering George W. Bush's nomination of John Ashcroft for attorney general, as a last resort. As much as I respected Ashcroft as a former senator with whom I had worked, his nomination tested my views about the degree to which a president is entitled to have his own people and advisors in place. We had the forty-one opposing votes necessary to filibuster Ashcroft. But out of respect for the fact that, like it or not, John Ashcroft had been one of our colleagues, we decided to allow his nomination to move to the floor, where he was eventually confirmed by a margin of 58–42. But that isn't how we came down on a lot of other nominees, especially lifetime judicial appointments, during the time that I was Leader.

Looking back, I would draw the distinction between judicial appointments and other kinds of nominations that have more limited timeframes, generally for the duration of the president's term, such as Cabinet secretaries. When a person is nominated to serve in a position for somewhere between two to four years, filibustering that person for more than a year, sometimes aided by secret holds, brings unfairness and dysfunction, to which we have to be more sensitive.

The position of attorney general, the nation's top law-enforcement officer, is the lone exception within the Cabinet. The attorney general, and operations of the Department of Justice, which he or she directs, must be kept free of ideological partisanship. A century ago, Theodore Roosevelt, a Republican president, heard rumors that some district attorneys and marshals would soon receive orders to replace their deputies for political reasons. Roosevelt immediately wrote to his attorney general, demanding that those orders be stopped. As Roosevelt put it, "Of all the offices of the Government, those of the Department of Justice should be kept free from any suspicion of improper action on partisan and factional grounds."

I've seen the confirmation process from both sides of the dais. In early 2009, President Obama nominated me to serve as Secretary of Health and Human Services, as the new administration was stepping up its push to redraw the health care system for the first time in a century. The process got bogged down in the Finance Committee, which along with the HELP Committee was holding hearings on my nomination. In 2005, a close friend who was also a Democratic donor had offered to let me use his Washington-based driver. My friend lived in New York but had generously hired a widower to drive him when he was in Washington, paying the man full-time for part-time work, because the man was caring for a special-needs child and couldn't work full-time. Around the same time, I was adjusting to life in the private sector, after twenty-six years in Congress, keeping a full schedule by patching together several new roles, as a special policy advisor at a law firm, working on health care issues at a think tank, and teaching at Georgetown. If my friend didn't need the driver most of the time, anyway, and the driver could fit in my trips around his daughter's needs, the arrangement should work well for everyone. It was a completely casual arrangement between friends, I thought, and that was all that mattered.

Several years later, when the president nominated me, the Finance Committee wanted to know why I hadn't reported the driving services as income for three years and paid taxes on them. Actually, I *had* paid the back taxes—which was what caught the committee's attention. For years, it had never crossed my mind that the driving might carry tax implications. However, when I was being vetted for the HHS nomination, we had to look at every possible tax issue from every possible angle. We decided that we had a close call in which different people might come to different conclusions, but that the safest move was amending my returns to count the driving services as income for all three years.

There were other issues, too. For example, my wife and I could no longer count some of our charitable contributions as deductions because we had mistakenly made the payment to the two directors of a South Dakota charity, rather than to the charity itself. We paid additional taxes to cover those expenses, too, and hoped that would clear up any remaining doubts and let my nomination go forward. But the Finance Committee kept asking questions, and it became clear that the issue wasn't going away. In the years since I had left the Senate in 2005, any old tensions with my Republican colleagues seemed to have faded away—until the Finance Committee's questions. Now I had become a polarizing figure, with one side of the aisle for me and one side against me. I might have been able to prevail after a lengthy political battle, but the last thing the new administration needed was to spend time and political capital on a troubled nomination. Plus, I would have started off wounded, with none of the bipartisan goodwill I had built up. The health care reform effort deserved better. To break through a hundred years of barriers, the White House needed someone who had the trust of lawmakers from both parties, who could help the administration listen to all sides and find the combination of changes that could pass Congress. I withdrew my name.

As a former senator, I understand the importance of what the Finance Committee was doing. They were providing congressional oversight of the new administration by scrutinizing the president's nominees. That's how Congress, at its best, can hold the executive branch to high ethical standards. Most people, though, don't realize the toll the process can take on nominees. You have to spend weeks poring over your finances in excruciating detail. Even those of us who have dealt with the tax code as policymakers can miss something in our personal finances. And mistakes can turn into raging scandals.[1]

Controversial and failed nominations draw the most attention, but the Senate has historically confirmed the vast majority of presidential choices, though it has rejected a third of Supreme Court nominees. But that limited success has been fading. The entire nominating system has grown dysfunctional, from the vetting, the number of nominees now subject to a vote, and the number of filibusters. In 2011, two extremely qualified people couldn't get nominated for key posts—Donald Berwick to run the Center for Medicaid and Medicare Services (CMS), and Elizabeth Warren to run the consumer protection bureau she had developed— not because of their abilities, but because of opposition to President Obama's legislative agenda.

Berwick was serving as CMS administrator under a "recess appointment," installed temporarily when the Senate was out of session. He resigned after forty-two Republican senators signed a letter pledging to block his confirmation. Warren, a Harvard professor, had spent a year setting up the Consumer Financial Protection Bureau (CFPB), but President Obama nominated another official, given Republican opposition to her.

In December 2011, Senate Republicans filibustered Caitlin Halligan, Obama's nominee to fill the vacancy that Chief Justice John Roberts had created on the D.C. Circuit Court when he advanced to the Supreme Court. Halligan did not seem to meet the standard of "extraordinary circumstances" to warrant a filibuster, set in a 2005 pact on judicial nominations by the bipartisan "Gang of Fourteen."

"It seems to me that a vote against this nominee is a vote that declares the Gang of Fourteen agreement null and void," Senator Chuck Schumer (D-N.Y.) said. "If Republicans are going to suddenly junk that six-year armistice, it could risk throwing the Senate into chaos on judicial nominees."[2]

The turmoil in late 2011 also threatened a "gentleman's agreement" struck early that year under which minority Republicans would filibuster fewer bills and nominations and majority Democrats would let Republicans offer more amendments. That agreement was part of a package of measures, including an effort to limit holds and to reduce the number of administration appointees who require Senate confirmation.[3] The 2011 pact addressed only filibusters on "motions to proceed," to bring a bill or a nomination to the Senate floor, not on filibusters to cut off debate on a bill and vote on final passage.

In recent decades, judicial confirmations have become battle royals over conservative efforts to change social policy by reshaping the faces and philosophy of the federal judiciary; to effect changes through the courts that conservative activists could not accomplish through Congress or the president, who are accountable to the people at the ballot box.

The modern trend began in the early 1980s. President Reagan, faced with a solidly Democratic House of Representatives, knew he couldn't advance his social agenda even through modest, incremental legislation. So he turned to the judiciary, to load the federal courts with conservative judges who would embrace and advance his social policies. Ever since, conservative activists have pressed Republican presidents for more like-minded appointments to the federal bench.

Reagan's nomination in 1987 of conservative appeals court judge Robert Bork, in particular, sparked a philosophical war, played out at top decibels by advocacy groups on both ends of the spectrum. Ted Kennedy may have set the tone, taking the Senate floor shortly after Reagan nominated Bork to declare:

> . . . Robert Bork's America is a land in which women
> would be forced into back-alley abortions, blacks would sit
> at segregated lunch counters, rogue police could break

down citizens' doors in midnight raids, schoolchildren could not be taught about evolution, writers and artists could be censored at the whim of the government, and the doors of the Federal courts would be shut on the fingers of millions of citizens.

Bork expounded at Judiciary Committee hearings on his theory of "original intent," that judges must hew to the Founders' views rather than adapting to changing times. Ultimately, the Judiciary Committee rejected Bork, followed by the full Senate, 42–58.

Later, George W. Bush often talked about seeking to nominate judges who were "strict constructionists," who viewed the Constitution as a literal document not to be interpreted by the court to deal with changing situations. Likewise, conservatives decry "judicial activists" on the bench—judges who use their rulings to push for social change.

Every American should care about the makeup of the federal judiciary. Federal judges serve for life, and their decisions can determine the interpretation—and even the constitutionality—of laws for decades. And once they're seated, the checks and balances are limited. As Chief Justice John Roberts said in 2010:

I think the most important thing for the public to understand is that we are not a political branch of government. They don't elect us. If they don't like what we're doing, it's more or less just too bad—other than impeachment, which has never happened, or a conviction on impeachment.[4]

Nominees for federal judgeships usually go through a long and demanding process. The FBI investigates their backgrounds and the American Bar Association formally rates them as well qualified, qualified, or unqualified. Nominees complete lengthy questionnaires from both the Department of Justice and the Senate Judiciary Committee. They then testify at Judiciary Committee hearings—technically, they can refuse the committee's invitation, but that would be unwise. The Judiciary Committee then votes on the nomination and either advances it to the Senate floor, with or without recommendation, or rejects it. Nominations, like other matters on the executive calendar, may then be called for debate and votes by the full Senate.

Too often, judicial nominees face long, politically driven delays at various stages of the process and may never get a hearing or a vote. Opponents often use holds to delay and defeat nominations. When Republicans controlled the Senate, we were often appalled at the treatment of many of President Clinton's nominees, just as Republicans were later appalled at the treatment of George W. Bush's nominees, which spurred their "Justice for Judges Marathon" talkathon. Fifty-seven Clinton nominees never got a Judiciary Committee hearing, and many more waited hundreds of days; some waited years. The political delays and defeats devastate not only the nominees, but the entire judicial system, creating a climate that discourages qualified candidates from accepting nominations and leaving courts dangerously understaffed.

Nominations, like nearly everything else in the Senate, rarely proceed in a vacuum, considered solely on their merits. Payback often plays a part. A years-long battle over a nominee for a federal appeals court seat, Charles Pickering of Mississippi, a close personal friend of Trent Lott, offers a good example. As Lott had told me, "There are times when you have to have something for your state, and there are times when I have to have something for mine." But Pickering, as a federal district judge, had opposed women's rights, civil rights, and lawsuits regarding employment discrimination. Ethical questions and evidence mounted during the confirmation process. Pickering's nomination was for a lifetime appointment one step below the Supreme Court, and the judge was clearly outside the mainstream. To me, Pickering's nomination grew beyond an issue of home-state importance to Lott. The matter came to a head between us during a rare joint interview on *Meet the Press* when, in response to a direct question from the moderator at the end, I hurt Lott's friend's chances. Lott felt blindsided by my candor at that interview. We spoke about it afterward, and I think he smarted for a while.

Lott retaliated, including taking the surprising action of blocking a $1.5 million appropriation to the Judiciary Committee to investigate terrorism. He said that since the Judiciary Committee wasn't processing judges, it didn't need the money. Lott also placed a hold on the nomination of one of my staff members for a seat on the Federal Communications Commission.

In February 2004, President Bush gave Pickering a recess appointment, and then did the same for another controversial appeals court nominee, William Pryor of Alabama, whom Democrats had also filibustered. The recess appointments put Pryor and Pickering on the appeals courts for the duration of the 108th Congress, until 2005, not for life. (As events worked out, Pryor would win formal Senate confirmation in 2005 through the Gang of Fourteen pact.) But these recess appointments crossed a line.

In March 2004, Democrats vowed no further action on judicial nominees unless Bush promised no further recess appointments. "We will be clear," I said on the Senate floor. "We will continue to cooperate in the confirmation of federal judges, but only if the White House gives the assurance that it will no longer abuse the process."

The president refused. And Republicans took the Senate to the brink of the nuclear option.

☆ 39. IMPEACHMENT ☆

In the ultimate check on power among the branches, Congress has the constitutional authority to remove executive and judicial branch officials from office. The Constitution states: "The President, Vice President, and all Civil Officers of the United States, shall be removed from office on Impeachment for, and Conviction of, Treason, Bribery, or other high Crimes and misdemeanors." The phrase "high crimes and misdemeanors" is vague, intended to cover a wide variety of offenses.

The two-step removal process begins when the House, by majority vote, impeaches an official, equivalent to issuing an indictment. The impeached official then goes before the Senate for trial, with House members serving as managers, or prosecutors. When a president is impeached, the chief justice presides at the trial, because the vice president would ascend to president upon conviction.

The full Senate, or an ad hoc appointed committee of senators, serves as jurors. The Senate has not created standing rules of evidence and other procedures for impeachment, which is why we had to work out those rules for President Clinton's trial. A two-thirds vote of senators present is required for conviction. Upon conviction on one count, the official will be removed from office, and no votes on additional charges are necessary. The Senate may then vote on whether to disqualify the official from again holding public office. On such a vote, a simple majority is required. Impeachment carries only one penalty—removal from office. But a convicted official remains liable for civil or criminal prosecution.

In our nation's history, the House has impeached seventeen officials, including Presidents Andrew Johnson and Bill Clinton, and the Senate has convicted seven. Several of those cases carried enormous consequences for the country.

In 1805, the Senate tried Supreme Court Justice Samuel Chase, a former member of the Continental Congress who had signed the Declaration of Independence. Chase was also a Federalist, and advocated a strong central government and due process. President Thomas Jefferson, leader of the Republicans (not the same party as the modern-day version), disliked the idea of lifetime appointments for judges, fearing the judiciary might grow too powerful. When Chase voiced Federalist views from the bench, Jefferson encouraged the House to impeach him.

Chase's case would determine whether judges could be ousted merely for their political views. If Jefferson could get rid of Chase, other Federalist judges, notably Chief Justice John Marshall, would probably follow. The Senate acquitted Chase, with unlikely help from Jefferson's own vice president, Aaron Burr, who ran a fair trial.[1] The Senate's wisdom set a precedent against impeaching judges for their political views, safeguarding the judiciary's independence.

In 1868, the Senate tried President Andrew Johnson in a case that grew over the president's struggle with Congressional Republicans over post–Civil War reconstruction of the South. Johnson was charged with violating the Tenure of Office Act, passed the previous year. He had removed Secretary of War Edwin Stanton and even appointed a successor, but Stanton had refused to resign, barricading himself in his office. Johnson's opponents insisted that the Senate would have to relieve Stanton, just as they had to confirm him. Republicans held more than a two-thirds majority in the Senate, so Johnson seemed headed for conviction. But seven Republican senators defected, unwilling to hobble the presidency. The Senate acquitted Johnson by a single vote, cast by a courageous freshman from Kansas, Edmund Ross, whose valor would earn him a chapter nearly a hundred years later in John F. Kennedy's *Profiles in Courage*.

The Clinton impeachment was the climax of Republican attacks on the president. As we've discussed, Trent Lott and I both recognized that the fabric of our nation might be torn beyond repair if the Senate trial degenerated into the same spectacle as the House impeachment. We agreed that was too high a price for a political victory, for either side.

The Constitution also provides a procedure for Congress to remove its own members: "Each House [of Congress] may determine the Rules of its proceedings, punish its members for disorderly behavior, and, with the concurrence of two-thirds, expel a member."

In its history, the Senate has expelled fifteen of its own, and fourteen of those were charged with supporting the Confederacy during the Civil War. More often, senators accused of various forms of corruption have resigned before the Senate began or completed formal expulsion proceedings.

Members of Congress do enjoy some special protections through the Constitution's "speech and debate" clause. That provision, which stems from struggles between the British king and parliament, aims to prevent the executive from interfering with legislative business by prohibiting prosecution of members of Congress for statements they make in debate and from arrest on their way to a session of Congress. Some recent criminal cases involving members of Congress have tested that point, where evidence was gathered or found at least partially on congressional property.

☆ 40. DECLARING WAR ☆

Only Congress can declare war—the Constitution is explicit on that point. Sending young Americans into harm's way may be the most important act of Congress, and a senator's most important decision. During war, the president serves as commander in chief; the Constitution is equally explicit about that. But in recent decades, American forces have repeatedly entered hostilities without formal declarations of war as presidents have flexed their military muscles, and the issue of when the president can assume his commander-in-chief role has created enormous strife between the branches.

The United States has not formally declared war since World War II. The Korean War set the modern precedent of conflict without formal declaration. In 1950, North Korea invaded South Korea, and President Truman sent in U.S. troops, at the United Nations' request, to repel the communists. At the time, Congress was in recess. The Vietnam War was also not a declared conflict, but Congress in August 1964 did pass the Gulf of Tonkin

Resolution, which gave President Lyndon Johnson the authority to help any Southeast Asian country deemed in peril of "communist aggression." Johnson used that joint resolution to justify military action that quickly escalated into full, open warfare. I served three years during that conflict as an Air Force intelligence officer.

In 1973, toward the end of the Vietnam War, Congress passed the War Powers Resolution to require presidents to seek congressional authorization for military action, except in cases of "a national emergency created by attack upon the United States, its territories or possessions, or its armed forces." The resolution spells out precise timeframes for the president to notify Congress and for withdrawing troops if Congress does not authorize an action. Congress passed the resolution over a veto, and presidents have often resisted and sometimes disregarded it since.

The first President Bush considered the 1991 Senate vote authorizing him to use "any means necessary" to liberate Kuwait, in what would become known as Gulf War I, the most important vote of his presidency. He reflected:

> Prior to the commencement of Desert Storm, we honored Congress' right to be heard, and to cast their votes, before a single shot was fired. In ending the war when we did, after Kuwait had been liberated, we also kept our word to our coalition partners—and abided by the international authority under which we agreed to operate. Our principled leadership and restraint enhanced our credibility in the region, and earned us a windfall of political capital—which we, in turn, used to jump-start the peace process.[1]

After the September 11 attacks, Congress agreed that a Use of Force authorization was required, and that we would provide one.

Whoever the attackers were, we would do all in our power to find them and bring them to justice. President George W. Bush asked for authorization to use military force and also to expand law enforcement officials' authority to meet this new threat. Especially in those first days of unity and common purpose after the attacks, there was no disagreement about our changed circumstances, but there was skepticism about providing new authority without limits on either scope or time.

After frenetic discussions with the White House and with congressional Republicans, many of whom shared our concerns that the president's proposed resolution was too far-reaching, we agreed on language that gave the president the authority he needed, but with limits. We wanted him to focus on those responsible for September 11.

I soon developed concerns that the president had exceeded that authority, and that scope. Specifically, Congress never authorized the administration to spy on Americans, which was why the administration tried to insert that specific authority into the resolution minutes before the Senate vote—and I turned them down. But then, it turned out, the administration ran a domestic eavesdropping program, anyway, claiming the resolution gave them implicit congressional authorization.

A president's responsibility to work with Congress does not end after Congress gives him the authority to use force—which I felt important to remind George W. Bush. When President Bush turned his scope toward Iraq, we wanted continuing consultation from him and assurance that his team was planning for a post-Saddam Iraq. To me, ongoing consultation with Congress was particularly important because I still had doubts about the imminence of the threat posed by Saddam Hussein.[2]

Congress's only fallback position is the power of the purse.

If lawmakers chose not to fund a military activity, it would cease. It is a powerful tool. In recent years, for example, all funding for abortions in military hospitals has been eliminated. There have also been provisions to eliminate funds for certain domestic intelligence activities.

☆ 41. TREATIES ☆

The Senate alone has the authority to ratify treaties, which are agreements between the United States and one or more other nations. Specifically, the Constitution gives the president the "Power, by and with the Advice and Consent of the Senate, to make Treaties provided two thirds of the Senators present concur." Treaties have ended wars, reduced nuclear stockpiles, expanded trade, and shifted control of property. They have made enormous contributions to peace, prosperity, and security. They have also made and broken public careers.

The Treaty of Versailles in 1919, which set the terms for peace and reparations after World War I, proved one of the Senate's darkest moments. President Woodrow Wilson sailed to France to lead the U.S. delegation at the peace conference in Paris. Wilson had conceived of and pressed for a covenant for creating a League of Nations, a global body to pursue world peace, as part of the treaty and was essentially staking his presidency on it.

The Paris conference produced a treaty that pleased Wilson, but the Senate would have to ratify it by two-thirds vote, and

Republicans had recaptured control of the Senate in 1918. The new Majority Leader and Foreign Relations Committee Chairman was Henry Cabot Lodge of Massachusetts, and Lodge and Wilson loathed each other. Wilson called Lodge and other Republican senators "contemptible, narrow, selfish, poor little minds that never get anywhere but run around in a circle and think they are going somewhere." Lodge, for his part, felt Wilson was trying to weaken the Senate by destroying its power over treaties.[1]

Wilson had not included a single senator among the five-member negotiating team he took to the Paris peace conference, and continued to believe he could impose his will on the Senate. Lodge's Foreign Relations Committee added fourteen "reservations" to the treaty—essentially, amendments aimed at protecting U.S. sovereignty.

Lodge stalled the treaty in committee while he orchestrated a massive public relations campaign to convince the American people, who initially favored the treaty, that a League of Nations would cripple U.S. sovereignty. Wilson launched his own PR counteroffensive, barnstorming the nation, exhausting himself to the point that he suffered two strokes, the second leaving him paralyzed and nearly blind. Still the president refused to negotiate, and in the end, in November 1919, the Senate defeated Lodge's fourteen reservations. But the Senate also rejected the Versailles Treaty, the first time the U.S. Senate had ever rejected a peace treaty.

Historian Robert Caro wrote: "The Senate's victory over the Treaty of Versailles proved again that the powers given that body by the Founding Fathers were strong enough to stand against the power of the executive and the power of public opinion—strong enough to stand, if necessary, against both at once."[2] But Caro called the rejection a "tragedy," writing that the treaty might have united the world and prevented the ascent of Hitler and Mussolini, and the war and horrors that followed.

PART
5

LIFE IN THE SENATE

42. BUSINESS ON A HANDSHAKE

It's often said—though not always true—that your word is your bond; that a handshake is as good as a signature. Generally, that's exactly how it works in the Senate. As the first President Bush said, "There aren't many places where you can still do business on a handshake, but you can still do it in the United States Senate."[1] Or as Senator Dole put it, "As we all learn around here, if you don't keep your word, it doesn't make much difference what agenda you try to advance."[2]

When Ted Kennedy died in August 2009, Senator Lindsey Graham, a South Carolina Republican, posted a short statement on his Web page about the tough negotiator from the other side of the aisle: "A handshake from Senator Kennedy was all that was ever needed. His word was his bond." That was high praise.

In the Senate, you fight daily on issues, but there's also an appreciation of the personal relationships you need to make this government work. Politicians generally like to like people and like to be liked, so you usually get through all of that. But sometimes a handshake proves inadequate, and you feel a sense of personal betrayal. I can recall a couple of those occasions. Somebody committed something to me, made a promise. We shook hands. I looked the person straight in the eye in my office, and then later they changed their opinion. The Senate works only if you have a sense of truthfulness and respect for one's word. When a handshake doesn't hold up, bonds rupture. But that's still a fairly rare event.

43. PRESS AND PRESSURES

☆ ☆

In 1859, Abraham Lincoln said, "Public opinion in this country is everything."[1] That statement, and the concept of an elected leader's legitimacy through ongoing public confidence, goes to the heart of democracy. That is, a politician or a major piece of legislation won't get far or last long without public support. That's why presidents and Senate leaders trumpet their "electoral mandates," and why they take and watch opinion polls.

In our country, through our constitutionally protected free press, the media generally shape public opinion. News reports can help pass a bill or vault a senator to reelection or to even higher office. Or prompt a filibuster or force a resignation or even an impeachment. Even in the twenty-first century, in the Internet age of blogs and e-mail and Facebook and Twitter and texting, the so-called Mainstream Media—established print and broadcast outlets and, yes, their online versions—still play the biggest role in informing the public and in shaping its views. Unfortunately, when it comes to that sausage-like business of making laws, disagreements and fights among senators and Senate leaders often make news, while so much gets done that doesn't draw ink or airtime that people oftentimes get the wrong impression.

For senators, the media offer the best conduit to their constituents. Senators and other elected officials often forge close relationships with the journalists who cover them. The senators want to land online mentions, ink, and airtime, and the reporters and producers want access to decision makers and they want news.

The framers did not envision such a cozy relationship. The media perform a public service as an adversary to the establishment, a check on power, a watchdog, with protections enshrined in the First Amendment and in later case law. Practiced at its highest level, journalism identifies systemic flaws, whether because of nonfeasance, malfeasance, or simply because of social or technological change, with an eye toward correcting them. That's why Thomas Jefferson famously said he would prefer newspapers without government to government without newspapers.

The pendulum has shifted in recent decades, especially since the *Washington Post*'s Watergate coverage, toward more vigorous investigation and exposure of public officials. The days are gone when reporters milled among lawmakers at Georgetown salons observing unwritten rules not to report drunken breaches of protocol or a president's disability or trysts. But media watchdogs can still become lapdogs, pulling punches in the interest of staying in a senator's good graces.

Generally, a senator keeps at least one eye on the media in much of what he does, says, and writes. As Donald Matthews wrote half a century ago:

> In order to survive, most senators must make news by the reporters' definition of the term. . . . Most of what is said on the Senate floor is aimed at making news via the press

galleries. Congressional investigations, too, are more often calculated to affect tomorrow's headlines than the statute books.[2]

A senator with legislative or political ambitions must maintain a presence both in the local press back home, generally through Washington correspondents and appearances on local radio and TV shows, on-site or remote; and in the national press, through the major media outlets with bureaus and reporters in Washington, and the national talk shows. Sunday morning network public affairs shows are the news vehicles of choice for national messaging.

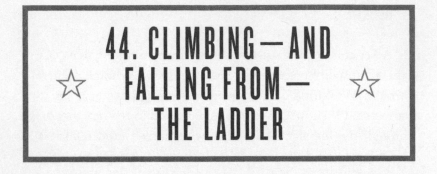

44. CLIMBING — AND FALLING FROM — THE LADDER

While lawmakers occasionally expel or force out one of their own, the career mortality rate among congressional leaders far outstrips that of rank-and-file members. On the House side in recent years, Jim Wright, Newt Gingrich, and Bob Livingston—before he even took office—all lost the Speakership amid scandal. On the Senate side, my counterpart Trent Lott stepped down as Republican Leader after making remarks widely seen as racially insensitive, touting Strom Thurmond's 1948 Dixiecrat presidential campaign. In my case, I lost my leadership position, along with my Senate seat, after a tough campaign.

There's an old axiom that the higher up the ladder you climb, the more exposed your rear becomes. You become more of a political target. That was certainly true in my case. There's no way to be sure, but my assumption has always been that, had I not been Leader, I might still be in the Senate today. In many respects, I'm glad I'm not.

As a Senate leader, you become, much like the president, a far richer target. Just about anybody who takes that role would be well advised to check the thickness of their hide before they do it, because it's not for the faint of heart. And it's certainly not for those who are unprepared for the criticism, the scrutiny, and the attacks against Senate leadership. Nobody was immune. Bob Dole took it. Howard Baker told me that he hit the height of negative feelings after the Panama Canal Treaty, which transitioned control of the canal to Panama by 1999.

The slings and arrows just come with the territory. You're not even surprised by the decibel level, because it rises gradually. It just creeps up on you, like rising temperature in a cauldron, and eventually you find yourself in boiling water. You look back and see how it happened, and you're just amazed.

☆ 45. TECHNOLOGY ☆

Advances in technology, especially in communications, have profoundly changed Senate life and operations. But the Senate did not always immediately embrace such advents.

In the spring of 1930, the Senate passed a resolution to replace its dial telephones—those were the days before push-button phones—with manual phones that relied on operators to make connections. The resolution stated that dial telephones were more difficult to operate than manual telephones and forced senators "to perform the duties of telephone operators in order to enjoy the benefits of telephone service." A day before the dial phones were scheduled to go, a senator offered a resolution to give members a choice, since some younger senators seemed to prefer the dial devices. Antidial senators blocked the measure. In the end, the telephone company provided phones that worked both ways.

In 1978, the Sergeant at Arms delivered the first computers to each Senate office. "A year later," historian Donald Ritchie said, "he came back and ninety of them were still in the boxes they were delivered in, because the Senators were too busy, their staff didn't want to bother learning how to use them, had to coax them into [it]. Now, they're addicted to them."

Even some journalists climbed slowly into the twentieth and twenty-first centuries. In 1990, the Senate press gallery removed its last telegraph machine. Until then, some reporters were still typing their stories and telegraphing them to their newspapers. Today, of course, everything is digital and electronic.

These days, Ritchie said, "as quickly as new technology develops, members adopt it, especially younger members and those in the minority." Senators have turned their Web sites into electronic newsletters replete with online surveys, and virtual town meetings, he noted. "Not that long ago, it was a different world."

Early in my congressional career, the advent of televised Senate proceedings brought a profound change. For starters, when C-SPAN began live floor coverage in 1986, the Senate amped up the lighting to accommodate the cameras, literally bringing the Senate from darkness to light. The chamber had been so dim, Robert Caro wrote, "when lights had not yet been added for television and the only illumination came from the ceiling almost forty feet above the floor . . . that its far end faded away in shadows."[1]

But more fundamentally, as we've noted, before cameras, if you wanted to know what was going on, you really had to be in the chamber. Beginning in the 1970s, squawk boxes could let you hear the proceedings, but to get a feel for the action, to know when your bill was coming up, a lot more senators and a lot more reporters gathered around the floor. Today, the only senators in the chamber are usually those signed up to speak, or who have to preside. The others are back in their offices, with their sets tuned to the floor. Reporters have also now mostly abandoned their chamber gallery for their offices and nearby press galleries.

At this writing, Senate leaders are deciding whether to allow personal electronic devices, such as BlackBerrys and iPhones, on the floor. The House has allowed the devices, but senators are doing it surreptitiously, hiding them under their desks, historian Ritchie said. "When Senator Byrd would come in the chamber, they would all put their BlackBerrys away."

I occasionally get e-mail messages from senators on the floor. And all Senate security messages, all votes and all messages from leadership are now transmitted through members' handheld devices.

The reason for the ban on using devices on the floor, according to legislative expert Walter Oleszek, is to keep the Senate chamber a sanctuary from the pervasive electronic chatter outside. The floor, he said, is supposed to be where senators come and listen to what colleagues have to say. Oleszek said the bigger issue is how you enforce the ban. If a senator brought a laptop into the chamber, as at least one asked to do, Leaders might object. But who would tell the presiding officer to holster his BlackBerry?[2]

46. WOMEN IN THE SENATE

The arrival of women as elected senators began relatively recently. Today, women's ranks in the Senate have grown to the point that several states are represented solely by women. But the advance was slow, gradual, and not always smooth.

In 1916, the first woman won election to Congress when Jeannette Rankin, a Montana Republican, won a House seat. A tireless campaigner for world peace who opposed U.S. entry into both World Wars, she lost a reelection battle in 1918 but returned to the House in 1940.

On October 3, 1922, America got its first female senator when Georgia governor Thomas Hardwick appointed eighty-seven-year-old Rebecca Felton to a vacant seat. Hardwick's motives were not entirely enlightened and altruistic. The governor wanted to run for the open Senate seat in November, but had alienated many of the state's new female voters a couple of years earlier by opposing ratification of the Nineteenth Amendment, which granted women the right to vote. By appointing Felton, Hardwick figured he could score points with the new women voters and avoid creating a rival in the upcoming general election. Felton was an established suffragist, but she wasn't a beacon of enlightenment, either, at least by today's standards. A champion of temperance, she also pressed for racial segregation as an outspoken white supremacist. In the end, Hardwick's scheme did him little good when he lost the general election to a Democrat.

In 1932, Hattie Caraway of Arkansas became the first woman to win election to the Senate. A year earlier, Caraway had been appointed to the seat after the death of her husband, the incumbent. Party leaders assumed—wrongly—that she wouldn't run for a full term. Caraway later became the first woman to preside over the Senate and to chair a committee, and served until 1945. When reporters asked Caraway how she felt presiding over the Senate in her 1943 milestone, she said, "Nothing to it," calling the Senate the "best behaved crowd of men you ever saw."

Maybe so, but institutional sexism lingered in the Senate, and at large. As late as the early 1950s, female staffers weren't allowed on the Senate floor. At one point in the late 1940s, a crisis hit and Majority Leader Scott Lucas's secretary ran onto floor to give him a message. "And there was this sort of shock," historian Ritchie said. "Women were not supposed to come onto the floor."

In 1948, Margaret Chase Smith, a four-term House member from Maine, caught the sexism head-on when she ran for the Senate. The wife of one of her opponents asked, "Why [send] a woman to Washington when you can get a man?" The misogynist attacks ultimately backfired in Maine, where women comprised two thirds of registered voters. In the Republican primary, Smith won twice as many votes as all her challengers combined, and went on to serve twenty-four years in the Senate.

After Smith left office in 1973, the Senate was without a single woman for six years. Until 1992, "The Year of the Woman," the Senate never had more than two women among its ranks at the same time. The 1992 watershed stemmed from the 1991 Senate confirmation hearings of Justice Clarence Thomas, in which law professor Anita Hill, an African-American woman, presented and defended her charges of sexual harassment before a Judiciary Committee composed entirely of white men. The committee, followed by the full Senate, ultimately confirmed Thomas.

In the 1992 elections, voters sent four women to the Senate, including Dianne Feinstein and Barbara Boxer, making California the first state with an entirely female Senate delegation. Barbara Mikulski, a Maryland Democrat, was happy enough for the company, but didn't care for the phrase "Year of the Woman." She said, "Calling 1992 the Year of the Woman makes it sound like the Year of the Caribou or the Year of the Asparagus. We're not a fad, a fancy, or a year."

Mikulski was prescient. As of this writing, seventeen sitting U.S. senators are women, among thirty-nine in our nation's history. They chair committees and hold leadership roles in both parties. And half the Senate staff is female. But until not that long ago, women were always an afterthought.

Women have brought a transformation. They've been somewhat unconventional, by traditional Senate standards, in their relationships and approach. Today, we're in a much more polarized environment, you can almost say, except for the women. They still socialize; they go to each other's homes for dinners and events. A lot of female senators, regardless of ideology and party, face a lot of the same demands, including having to tend to young children in a way that men—for whatever reasons—don't. They have a sisterhood that transcends political and ideological differences. And so there's a camaraderie among Senate women that defies the current circumstances, almost to a person.

Senator Kirsten Gillibrand, a New York Democrat with young children, has been pressing to increase women's numbers in the Senate and throughout government. "We tend to be more results-oriented and less concerned with getting the credit," she told *The New York Times*. "The female approach is more conciliatory and less combative. We tend to use a more civil tone."[1]

From that perspective of civility and bipartisanship, women have been an inspiration to the rest of the Senate. I only wish we men had their secret, or their formula.

Some of the transformation is striking—visually. Men tend to be very conservative dressers, while women often dress more colorfully. Look at the audience at a State of the Union message and you'll see all the men in dark suits and many of the women in bright primary colors. I think that's also a very positive contribution to Senate environment.

The couture awakening came in the late 1980s, by Donald Ritchie's account. In the years before 1992, when the women's caucus was just Mikulski and Kansas Republican Nancy Kassebaum, they wore muted colors—Kassebaum was usually in beige, while Mikulski dressed to blend in. An unwritten rule barred women from wearing slacks in the Senate. All that changed one Saturday in the late 1980s. For that session, the women noted that the men were all going to be dressed casually. Female staffers talked the women senators into wearing slacks that Saturday, and every woman who showed up on the Senate floor was wearing slacks. "And none of the men had the nerve to say anything about it," Ritchie said. "And that was it. From that point on, women could wear pants, slacks, dresses, whatever."[2]

Today, several states have two female senators: Feinstein and Boxer still represent California, joined by all-female delegations in Washington and Maine. It's also encouraging that not only "blue states" have sent two women; both Maine senators are Republicans.

When I was Leader, advancing women was always a consideration, and an important statement that our caucus needed to make. Barbara Mikulski was a member of the leadership team from the very beginning, in part because I wanted to make sure that both women and men were in leadership. After that, Hillary Clinton became the Steering and Outreach chair. Patty Murray of Washington was Democratic Senatorial Campaign Committee chair. Barbara Boxer has long been a member of the leadership team, and chief deputy whip since 2005.

Because of established gender roles in our culture, women are expected to be treated somewhat differently, but Mikulski, for one, does not play a deferential role. Mikulski can be a bombastic and incredibly colorful speaker with a very authoritative voice. She introduced us to an old dance hall that serves German food and plays old-time music, Blob's Park in Jessup, Maryland, about halfway between Washington and Baltimore. She asked me to dance, and she led. She has an aura about her that just invokes authority, even though she's small in stature. As *The New York Times* described her, "At four foot eleven, she is the shortest member of the body, and is widely considered one of its toughest."[3] Nobody ever challenged Mikulski, or gave her any guff, or in any way minimized her role. They knew that crossing her was just not well advised. And so I thought she was the perfect pioneer.

With the ascent of women in the Senate, another matter that became a bit of an issue was what you call a woman senator. Is it Madam Chair? Do you still say Chairman? Is it Chairwoman? Is it Madam President, when you address the presiding officer?

The semantic adjustment, especially for senators who'd been around a long time, presented a challenge. Robert Byrd, our keeper of institutional history and decorum, who had been in the Senate since 1959, expressed to me a little intimidation, not knowing the appropriate nomenclature, having to think about it. Over time, most senators became familiar and comfortable with the new titles. It's "Madam President," for example, when a female senator presides.

The House has about the same share of women among its ranks as the Senate, 72 out of 435 at this writing, including Minority Leader Nancy Pelosi, a California Democrat who became the first female Speaker of the House in January 2007.

☆ 47. DIVERSITY ☆

The Senate has made progress on racial and ethnic inclusiveness, but still doesn't have the diversity that I wish it had. A democracy and a republic that's well represented should have diversity that reflects its society. Still, senators put a lot of effort into doing the best they can to reflect their constituencies. Democrats, as a party, trust diversity and encourage and embrace it as a fundamental tenet of our society, and feel enriched and strengthened by the differences among us. Sure, Democrats are probably a bit more empathetic partly because diverse groups comprise our constituency, but the feeling is genuine, and strong.

At this writing, the Senate has two Hispanic members, Robert Menendez (D-NJ) and Marco Rubio (R-Fla.), and two Asian American members, Daniel Inouye and Daniel Akaka, both from Hawaii. But with the departures of now-President Obama and his successor, Roland Burris, both Illinois Democrats, there are no African American members.

Diversity is greater in the House, where smaller, more homogenous districts often send representatives to Washington who reflect their demographics, just as House members often reflect more extreme positions on the issues. Forty-one African Americans now serve in the House. The House also has Buddhist and Muslim members.

Drive around the Capitol complex today, and you'll find your path blocked by barricades and armed guards on a frustrating number of streets. Walk through the complex, especially toward the Capitol, and you'll find many corridors closed or blocked. The new Visitor Center is a wonderful and important addition, but the public's limited access to the Capitol proper is an unfortunate reality of twenty-first-century life.

The new security measures came for good reason. The September 11 plot may have also targeted the Capitol, or perhaps the White House—either an unthinkable tragedy prevented by heroic passengers who tried to retake control of their hijacked airliner, ultimately giving their lives as Flight 93 crashed in rural Pennsylvania.

As late as the 1970s, tourists and other visitors could enter and wander through the Capitol whenever Congress was in session, almost without restriction. The only metal detectors then were by the Senate and House galleries. "You walked in and out of doors, you parked on the plaza; it was very casual," historian Ritchie recalled. "Citizens could wander at will through the building." That was my experience when I served as a Senate staffer during the 1970s, which gives me a more acute feel for just how much the environment has changed.

September 11 was not the first attack on the Capitol, if that was indeed Flight 93's target.

In March 1954, four extremist Puerto Rican nationalists opened fire with semiautomatic pistols from a visitors' gallery at the House chamber, firing thirty shots at the crowded floor during debate over an immigration bill and hitting five members. The gunmen unfurled a Puerto Rican flag and shouted, "Viva Puerto Rico libre!" to protest Puerto Rico's new constitution, which gave the U.S. Congress authority over the commonwealth. Authorities captured three of the gunmen immediately and the fourth later. They all received long prison terms.

In 1971, a bomb exploded in a Capitol restroom on the Senate side, causing an estimated $300,000 in damage but no injuries. A radical group that opposed the Vietnam War claimed responsibility.

Late one night in November 1983, a caller claiming to represent the "Armed Resistance Unit" warned the Capitol switchboard that a bomb had been placed near the chamber in retaliation for recent U.S. military involvement in Grenada and Lebanon. The Senate had planned to stay in session late that night, but wound up reaching agreement and adjourning early. Two minutes after the call, a bomb exploded under a bench, blowing off then-Democratic Leader Byrd's door; shredding a portrait of Daniel Webster; blowing a hole in a wall partition; and shattering mirrors, chandeliers, and furniture. Three members of the so-called Resistance Conspiracy ultimately got long prison terms.

In July 1998, a mentally ill man opened fire with a pistol, killing two Capitol Hill police officers, one of whom wounded the gunman before succumbing. The two policemen, Detective John Gibson and Officer Jacob Chestnut, lay in state in the Capitol rotunda. The gunman remains in a psychiatric institution.

In mid-October 2001, with America's wounds still raw a month after 9/11, the biggest bioterrorist attack in U.S. history hit: the anthrax letters. Anthrax is a lethal bacterium perfected for decades in military labs, among other places, and the batch that arrived at my Hart Building office was far more sophisticated and dangerous than the deadly spores sent a few weeks earlier to New York and Florida media outlets. Another letter addressed to Senator Pat Leahy, similar to the one sent to me, was found among quarantined mail. The months-long nightmare on Capitol Hill included taking nasal swabs from six thousand employees; other tests; quarantine; weeks of ingesting an antibiotic called Cipro; follow-up vaccines; shutdown of all House and Senate buildings for environmental testing; and then a months-long shutdown, sealing, and fumigation of the entire nine-story Hart Building, relocating fifty senators and thirteen committees. For two months, the nation lived in terror. In the end, five people died, though no congressional staff. To this day, authorities have not conclusively figured out who mailed those letters.

Each of those attacks ratcheted up Capitol and Senate security. Following the 1983 attack, ID cards were issued to staff and parts of the Capitol were cordoned off. Metal detectors were installed at all Capitol entrances and some sections of the building were restricted to those with official badges. The restrictions greatly increased after 9/11.

But despite all the metal detectors and blocked streets and corridors, the Capitol remains one of the most open public buildings in the government, Ritchie stressed. "It's harder to get into the most obscure cabinet office than it is to get into the U.S. Capitol. . . .

And that's because Congress wants its constituents to see it at work. Because its constituents are also its voters. . . . And communications and opening the place up to visitors are really critical parts of what they do."[1]

We all feel a heightened sense of threat in this post-September 11 world. I certainly felt invaded by the anthrax attack, getting targeted so directly and having so many others affected because of it. Every congressional leader gets death threats. One of those who sent me threats had a computer file on me and was actually arrested. Personally, I had made peace with such threats early during my time as Leader. After a Senate security assessment, I realized that if I worried as much as the security staff about my public exposure, I'd hardly be able to function. So I embraced a kind of fatalism, a willing acceptance that my time would come when it came and I couldn't live my life worrying about when that time might be. I expect most senators and congressmen feel the same way.

PART
☆ **6** ☆

THE SENATE TODAY,
AND TOMORROW

☆ 49. COMPROMISE ☆

Democrats and Republicans used to work together in the Senate and in Washington, until fairly recently. It was the work of government, and it was our *job* to do it. No matter how bitter the toe-to-toe fighting might sometimes become, you can never stop talking. For if you don't talk, you can't govern. And that, in the end, is your obligation as a public servant—not to win elections, but to do the work of government once you *do* win. Occasionally, the Senate still works well and when it does, it's news. *The New York Times* ran a story in May 2012, headlined, "With a Bipartisan Flurry, Becoming a Do-Something Senate," about a spate of passed legislation and confirmed nominees.

As leaders, Trent Lott—who succeeded Bob Dole—and I had to work together so often that we installed direct "hot line" phones in our offices so that each of us could reach the other to quickly work out issues that arose. For a time, Lott and I presided over the first evenly divided Senate since 1881. In introducing the organizing resolution in January 2001 for the only fifty-fifty Senate in the nation's history, I said on the floor:

I want to thank my friend, the Republican Leader, Senator Lott. Without his leadership and his sense of basic fairness, this agreement might not have come about. . . . Senator Lott and I have also discussed other ways to ensure bipartisanship in the Senate. . . . We have pledged to work together to make the Senate operate in a fair and bipartisan manner, which I hope will enable us to demonstrate to the American people that their system of government is strong and sound.

. . . We cannot quantify bipartisanship. Bipartisanship is not a mathematical formula. It is a spirit. It is a way of working together that tolerates open debate. It recognizes principled compromise—like today's historic agreement.

Compromise is key to bipartisanship, to cooperation, to getting things done. Politics—and, to a great extent, life—has been defined as the art of compromise. The Senate itself was borne of "The Great Compromise." As Henry Clay said, "All legislation is founded on the principle of mutual concession. Let him who elevates himself above humanity say, if he pleases, I never will compromise; but, let no one who is not above the frailties of our common nature disdain compromise."

50. ESCALATING PARTISANSHIP

President Gerald Ford, who had also presided over the Senate as vice president, lamented the increasing partisan rancor a quarter century after he left office. "Unfortunately," he said, "there are some on the right and some on the left for whom 'consensus' is a dirty word. A few mistake the clash of ideas for a holy war . . ."[1]

When partisanship becomes that divisive, it prevents passage of needed legislation and kills debate on vital public policy matters. In the decade since President Ford issued his warning, the partisanship has only grown worse. After leaving the Senate in 2005, I formed the Bipartisan Policy Center with former Senate Majority Leaders Dole, Mitchell, and Baker—two of us Democrats and two Republicans—to help bring centrist solutions and principled compromises. We began by encouraging civil, respectable discourse between the political parties, and have done some good and influential work.

But the political climate remains at a partisan boil. President Obama's 2009 stimulus plan, widely hailed as preventing an economic collapse, drew only three Republican crossovers in the Senate, and none in the House. Later that year, the president's health care plan drew no Republican votes at all. It's hard to imagine a bigger political challenge than finding real ways to cut back on health care spending that Americans take for granted, and that is why past administrations and Congresses failed to do so. But one side wouldn't even give the new president a chance. One Republican senator called health care the president's "Waterloo," referring to the 1815 battle in which British and allied forces effectively ended Napoleon's reign, and vowed that they would "break" Obama.

In February 2011, the federal government came within half an hour of shutting down in an impasse over legislation to continue funding federal operations. A few months later, an impasse over the federal debt limit threatened another shutdown. Though the sides again finally agreed on a temporary fix, the discord prompted a downgrade of U.S. debt and a stock market mini-crash.

Yes, there has always been partisanship in the Senate, and rancor, too. And some gridlock. More than a hundred years ago, President Theodore Roosevelt said, "Congress does from a third to a half of what I think is the minimum that it ought to do, and I am profoundly grateful that I get that much."

In the old days, the clashes sometimes grew violent, even deadly. In 1804, Vice President Aaron Burr shot and killed Treasury Secretary Alexander Hamilton in a duel. In 1854, Senators Thomas Hart Benton of Missouri and Henry Foote of Mississippi got into a spat on the Senate floor. Foote pulled a pistol on his bigger opponent. Benton hollered, "I have no pistols! Let him fire! Stand out of the way and let the assassin fire!" The Senate quickly adjourned, perhaps saving lives. In 1856, South Carolina Congressman Preston Brooks, incensed over the slavery issue and

Massachusetts Senator Charles Sumner's sharp abolitionist comments days earlier, charged onto the Senate floor and beat Sumner bloody and unconscious with a metal-tipped cane. In 1902, Senator John McLaurin of South Carolina on the Senate floor accused his state's senior senator, Ben Tillman, of making "a willful, malicious, and deliberate lie." Tillman spun around and punched McLaurin in the jaw. That led to a Senate rule that still stands: "No Senator in debate shall, directly or indirectly, by any form of words impute to another Senator or to other Senators any conduct or motive unworthy or unbecoming a Senator."[2]

But senators should be able to disagree without being disagreeable, to paraphrase the old saying. Not so long ago, senators seemed to take their partisan differences less personally.

John McCain and his wife, Cindy, invited my wife, Linda, and me to spend a weekend at their home near Sedona, Arizona, at a dicey time when I was talking to McCain about his changing parties, an effort Democratic leaders call "missionary work." I approached McCain on the Senate floor during a vote and said, "People are going to make a lot more of this than they should. Do you want to just cancel the trip?"

"Hell, no!" he said. "I want you guys to come as much now as before. Screw 'em."

So we did. And we drew protestors and headlines, but had a wonderful weekend.[3]

My biggest gesture of cross-party kinship was certainly "The Hug." Days after the terrorist attacks in September 2001, President George W. Bush addressed a joint session of Congress, House and Senate, and challenged the whole world to make a decision. "Either you are with us," he declared, "or you are with the terrorists." As President Bush stepped down from the dais and moved toward me, he reached out and we embraced. We looked at each other without saying a word, like brothers who understood the meaning of the moment. And at that moment, there wasn't a Democrat or a Republican in that room. There were only Americans.

But that moment lasted only so long. The Senate is not the "club" it was when I joined in 1987, when members forged lasting relationships, often across the aisle. And even those days were a world away from the Lyndon Johnson 1950s or the Mike Mansfield 1960s, when senators actually stayed in Washington over the weekend and socialized with one another rather than flying back to their home states or to some other distant spot.

51. THE SENATE'S SLIDE

In recent decades, the Senate has become both more partisan and more individualistic, losing some grace in the process. Many traditions, or folkways, are fading. Some of the old ways just don't fit in the twenty-first century. Senators no longer wait, out of deference and humility, sometimes for months, before making a maiden speech. That's fine, especially when Americans expect prompt action from every senator they send to Washington to tackle today's tough problems. But senators also commit far greater assaults on "comity," a favorite Senate term for courtesy and consideration of others. One plan to redraw the Senate rules to bull through nominations earned the name "the nuclear option" because it would vaporize every bipartisan bridge. Four major factors have brought profound changes to Congress and the Senate in recent decades:

First, the airplane: Air travel accommodates senators who feel the need to be in their states at least as much as they are in Washington. But if you're not in Washington, you can't address the problems, and you don't develop the social bonds that form when you live here and spend time together.

The lack of socialization has undermined senators' communications capacity. It has also created an attitude that to live in Washington is a bad thing, which conjures a sense that the nation's capital is foreign territory, where our representatives don't want to be comfortable. My own congresswoman from South Dakota, newly elected, made quite a statement when she first arrived: "A lot of us freshmen don't have a whole lot of knowledge, necessarily, about the way that Washington, D.C., is operated. And frankly, we don't really care."[1]

That's troubling. Because if you don't want to know how Washington works, it's pretty hard to make Washington work on behalf of the rest of the country.

Second, the money chase: The huge amount of money required to run for election in competitive states and congressional districts these days has required members to spend far too much of their time raising funds. My final Senate race cost some $25 million on either side, or $50 million in a small state like South Dakota.

So you find yourself on the phone "dialing for dollars" most of your time in the last two years of your term. You're raising money for ads, events, staff, travel, and other campaign expenses, instead of legislating, and it gives those who have the money enormous influence and access to members of Congress. The Supreme Court's 2010 *Citizens United* ruling, which took off all limits on corporate and union campaign spending, exacerbated the problem.

"The pressure of big money in politics and its power to compromise and destroy public trust still threaten the Senate and our nation," as former Senator and Vice President Walter Mondale put it.[2]

The third factor is how House districts have been redrawn in state legislatures every decade to accommodate either majority party by making "safe seats" for that party's nominees. That has made the primary election, to choose nominees, more important than the general election, to choose the winner from among the nominees. That drives candidates and congressmen more and more beholden to the bases on either side—to the less flexible, more doctrinaire party faithful. And in turn, more partisan House firebrands take their scorched-earth culture with them when they advance to the Senate. The practice of carving electoral districts for political advantage, sometimes in odd shapes, is known as "gerrymandering," named after early nineteenth-century Massachusetts Governor Elbridge Gerry, who used the technique on state senate districts.

The fourth factor is a dramatic change in the media, from the days when network television anchors Walter Cronkite and Tom Brokaw and people of stature reported the news in a fairly objective way, and newspapers observed a wall between news and editorial/opinion pages, and ran fairly unbiased stories. Now you have blogs, the Internet, and breathless, hyperbolic journalism that dramatically ratchets up the political pressures. The media have evolved from being political referees to political participants.

Whether it's Fox News on the right or MSNBC on the left, it's all news with a real slant today. And while newspapers generally are still objective in their reporting, people are not as exposed as they used to be to papers, which no longer provide their primary source of news.

All of those factors have created a combative and polarized political environment that, at least for the foreseeable future, doesn't provide any real expectation or hope that things will change. Those four factors seem so entrenched and permanent right now. Yet we know from experience that as permanent as things seem, they're always changing. So I'm hopeful.

52. THE PRICE OF PARTISAN GRIDLOCK

Honorable debate and compromise has been in rather short supply in the Senate these last few years. Its absence has prevented us from doing many things we ought to do. Meanwhile, Congress has sunk to record lows in public esteem. Business leaders cite the debt limit standoff and other impasses as destroying their confidence in their elected leaders and prompting them to reduce hiring, feeding our unemployment crisis. Such widespread disdain fuels public cynicism about government and the Senate, making it even harder to draw the public support needed to build coalitions to pass legislation. As my colleague Sen. Frank Lautenberg said:

> Democracy simply cannot function in atmosphere of distrust. After all, when citizens view everything the Congress does in the worst possible light, they are similarly skeptical about the legislation we propose. That makes it extremely difficult to build public support. And without public sup-

port, it becomes almost impossible to address major social problems in a meaningful way.[1]

We need a level of competence in government that allows us to address the serious and complex challenges we're facing today—energy issues, climate questions, budgetary issues, economic policy, joblessness, infrastructure challenges, health care, and education.

During the Clinton administration, I helped organize a "Health Care University" on Capitol Hill. Then-Majority Leader Mitchell and I feared that many of us weren't prepared to make decisions on the complex issues of health care, including who should provide which benefits. So we brought some of the best minds in the country to Washington to conduct workshops on various aspects of those issues. Members of both parties trooped around with yellow pads, "like students," as one newspaper described the scene. I don't know whether the Senate could hold such a "university" today.

The more our government grows dysfunctional and incapable of addressing these serious problems, the more the quality of life in America—and the vision of what America can be—suffers. And the consequences have global dynamics. The more dysfunctional we grow, the less competitive we will be in our aspirations internationally—economic, diplomatic, or even in terms of national security. The United States has gone from being interdependent to increasingly economically and socially integrated with the rest of world. And that integration requires a level of leadership and competence in governance that we're not demonstrating regularly these days.

Our nation, and our Senate, has long been a global beacon. In 1832, the French political and social observer Alexis de Toqueville visited the Senate and wrote that the body was "composed of eloquent advocates, distinguished generals, wise magistrates, and statesmen of note, whose arguments would do honor to the most remarkable parliamentary debates of Europe." It's unlikely that de Toqueville would report the same of today's Senate. And what message does democracy send the rest of world, when it's clear we can't solve our own problems any more effectively than we do?

If we're the standard by which other democracies and republics judge themselves, we've lowered the bar. And that's not helpful, especially with the world in as much transition as it is—in northern Africa, the Middle East, and other areas. It's vital for us to do a better job than we're doing today—and that must begin, as much as anywhere, in the Senate. Much of that work may soon fall to the next generation.

☆ 53. THE FUTURE ☆

This Congress has sunk to its lowest public approval rating since polling began, at 9 percent in one major survey, seen less favorably than the IRS and even Richard Nixon at the end of his presidency. Many Americans say that members of Congress are more interested in advancing their own fortunes, both political and financial, than they are in promoting the public interest; that lawmakers cater to the interests that finance their campaigns ahead of the citizens they represent. Scandals feed that cynicism, as a parade of elected officials faces charges of bribery, influence peddling, sexual misconduct, and other crimes. Some of the contempt is justified, and some is not, as we've seen.

While Americans may hold lawmakers in disdain, they maintain a high regard for the institutions of our government. Even so, the ongoing criticism of Congress and the Senate has been hard for me, because I so respect the institutions. Again, making law, by its nature, isn't always pretty. Imagine the degree of emotional investment in a lot of fights that you'd have with 300 million people, and that's what happens every day on the floor of the

U.S. Senate. I call it the noise of democracy. Sometimes it's not stereophonic, but it sure beats the noise of violence that erupts when decisions are made in a lot of other countries.

There is a way out of this predicament. Howard Baker said a few years ago, "It doesn't take Clays and Websters and Calhouns to make the Senate work. . . . Lotts and Daschles do it now. . . . The founders didn't require a nation of supermen . . . only honorable men and women laboring honestly and diligently and creatively in their public and private capacities."[1]

Ironically, even some of the founders lamented our government's talent pool. In 1774, John Adams wrote in his diary, "We have not men fit for the times. We are deficient in genius, education, in travel, fortune—in everything. I feel unutterable anxiety."[2] Still, we survived, and thrived.

Congress must begin by acknowledging some of its shortcomings. When it came to health care, Congress lacked professional expertise and trustworthiness, and generally admitted as much. Congress also has acknowledged its limitations in other fields, especially in the scientific sphere. Most of the time, politicians are wise enough not to incur on the turf of NIH medical researchers or NASA engineers. When they do, the results aren't often pretty.

In some other areas where Congress has such deficiencies, lawmakers have delegated power to quasi-independent entities composed of credible experts who were immune to political pressure. The Simpson-Bowles panel in December 2010 produced a credible framework for taming our government debt, though those prescriptions failed to gain threshold political support. A bipartisan "supercommittee" composed entirely of senators and House members took up the baton in 2011, but could not produce a plan, and formally admitted failure.

The independent commission model holds promise, as used in military base assessments and closures. The country needed those efficiencies and cost savings, but no lawmaker was eager to give up the jobs, revenue, and cachet that came from a military base in his or her district or state. So in 1988, Congress and the Pentagon devised the Base Realignment and Closure process, known as BRAC. Former lawmakers and retired military officers on the commission worked with Pentagon experts to craft a list of base closures and realignments. They then presented their list to the secretary of defense, who could either accept or reject it, but could not change it. Finally, the list went before Congress for a single up-or-down vote. In five rounds between 1988 and 2005, BRAC closed or shrank hundreds of bases and saved billions of dollars.

I have long advocated a structure similar to our federal reserve system for health care, as a way to create political insulation and greater expertise in decision making on health policy.

To break the gridlock, senators need to build relationships the way they used to. With solid personal foundations, lawmakers can more easily overcome political differences. Some ask how any relationship can survive the blood sport of national politics. The answer is, you've got to keep trying. You keep the dialogue open. Sometimes it required me to walk over to the Republican Leader's office, and vice versa—those leadership offices are only about fifty yards apart, but it's one of the longest walks you'll ever take. Sometimes, it's a matter of picking up the phone. And sometimes you sit and look at that phone for hours, off and on, and finally, you work up whatever it takes to pick up the handset and say, "Look, I want to clarify something. I want to say something more about whatever it is that was the cause of whatever trouble." And that's how you get through this.

I can't compare my work to anybody else's, but there were times when the tension and the depth of emotion were so high that you can't really explain it. All you can do is figure out a way to work through it, rise to the level people expect of you as a Leader, and try to do the nation's business the best you can.

I don't mind a good fight. I relish fighting when I have to, when I think it's absolutely critical for the country, and standing up for the things I believe. But I also relish the fact that Republicans and Democrats can work together, as they united to get through 9/11 and all those other travails over the decades. I worked with three Republican Leaders: Trent Lott, Bob Dole, and Bill Frist. And with each one, I would call it a good working relationship, in spite of our differences.

Some confrontation is actually healthy, because a good, civil, pro-con debate can shed as much light as heat. I think that confrontation with civility is exactly what our Founding Fathers had in mind. Unfortunately, sometimes we lose that civility, and that's where the problems begin. I don't think we should get along just to go along. It's important for us to debate, but there comes a time when you've got to move on and agree where you can and disagree where you have to.

Many observers paint politicians as driven by ambition, competitiveness, or hunger for power or fame. For my part, though I've been out of elective office for some years now, I would describe myself as driven more by restlessness to make a difference and by the need for a challenge. After I've worked at something for a long time, the restlessness begins to stir and I start looking for ways to make more of a difference in some new, different way.

I hope many of you will also feel the pull to serve and help steer our nation, perhaps in elective office, perhaps one day in the U.S. Senate. Keeping our republic always requires two things: fighting for it and working at it. With the right enlightened approach, our best days truly do lie ahead of us.

The writer Thomas Wolfe said that "America . . . is a place where miracles not only happen, but where they happen all the time."

☆ NOTES ☆

1. A CHAIN OF HISTORY

1. Senator Tom Daschle with Michael D'Orso, *Like No Other Time* (New York: Crown Publishers, 2003), p. 267.

2. Mike Mansfield, Leader's Lecture, March 24, 1998, Washington, D.C.

2. MAKING HISTORY EVERY DAY

1. Donald Ritchie, interview with the author, August. 5, 2011. Washington, D.C. Tape-recorded.

2. Ibid.

4. BIPARTISANSHIP

1. "The Empty Chamber," by George Packer, *New Yorker*, August 9, 2010.

2. Ibid.

3. Robert J. Dole, Leader's Lecture, March 28, 2010. Washington, D.C.

4. Howard Baker, Leader's Lecture, July 14, 1998, Washington, D.C.

7. THE PEOPLE'S HOUSE AND THE UPPER HOUSE

1. Scot M. Faulkner, *Naked Emperors* (Maryland: Rowman & Littlefield, 2007), p. 85.

8. DIFFERENT STROKES

1. Senator. Harry Reid, *Congressional Record*, 110/1 (May 10, 2007), S5883.

2. John F. Kennedy, *Profiles in Courage* (New York: Pocket Books, 1956), p. 11.

9. CHECKS AND BALANCES

1. Donald Ritchie, interview with the author, August 5, 2011. Washington, D.C. Tape-recorded.

11. THE VP: PRESIDENT OF THE SENATE

1. Robert A. Caro, *Master of the Senate* (New York: Alfred A. Knopf, 2002), p. 1035–1040.

2. Walter Mondale, Leader's Lecture, September 4, 2002. Washington, D.C.

3. George H. W. Bush, Leader's Lecture, January. 20, 1999, Washington, D.C.

12. THE WORKERS AND THE WORKLOAD

1. Donald R. Matthews, *U.S. Senators and Their World* (New York: W. W. Norton & Company, 1973), p. 81.

2. Richard Reidel, *Halls of the Mighty* (Washington: Robert B. Luce), p. 97.

3. Donald R. Matthews, *U.S. Senators and Their World* (New York: W. W. Norton & Company, 1973), p. 90.

4. Arlen Specter with Charles Robbins, *Passion for Truth: From Finding JFK's Single Bullet to Questioning Anita Hill to Impeaching Clinton* (New York: William Morrow & Company, 2000), p. 277.

5. Neil MacNeil, *Dirksen: Portrait of a Public Man* (New York: The World Publishing Company, 1970), p. 97.

6. "10 of Truman's Happiest Years Spent in Senate," John W. McDonald, Independence Examiner Truman Centennial Edition / Truman Library & Museum, May 1984.

7. Walter Mondale, Leader's Lecture, September 4, 2002. Washington, D.C.

13. SENATE STAFF

1. Donald Ritchie, *The U.S. Congress: A Very Short Introduction* (New York: Oxford, 2010), p. 123.

2. Lisa Ackerman, Press Secretary—Senator Mark Pryor, telephone interview with the author, Washington, D.C., September 29, 2011.

16. LOADING FROGS INTO A WHEELBARROW

1. Howard Baker, Leader's Lecture, July 14, 1998, Washington, D.C.

2. Richard E. Cohen, "Sen. Mitchell, A Lame Duck, Sizes Up '94," *National Journal,* March 12, 1994, p. 598.

3. Donald R. Matthews, *U.S. Senators and Their World* (New York: W. W. Norton & Company, 1973), p. 127.

17. THE MAJORITY AND THE MINORITY

1. Mike Mansfield, Leader's Lecture, March 24, 1998, Washington, D.C.

2. Senator Tom Daschle with Michael D'Orso, *Like No Other Time* (New York: Crown Publishers, 2003), p. 23.

18. COMMITTEES

1. Donald R. Matthews, *U.S. Senators and Their World* (New York: W. W. Norton & Company, 1973), p. 167.

19. COMMITTEE CHAIRS

1. Walter J. Oleszek, *Congressional Procedures and the Policy Process, Seventh Edition* (Washington: CQ Press, 2007), p. 92.

2. Donald R. Matthews, *U.S. Senators and Their World* (New York: W. W. Norton & Company, 1973), p. 162.

20. SENATE RULES

1. Walter Mondale Leader's Lecture, September 4, 2002. Washington, D.C.

2. Donald Ritchie, interview with the author, August 5, 2011. Washington, D.C. Tape-recorded.

3. Donald R. Matthews, *U.S. Senators and Their World* (New York: W. W. Norton & Company, 1973), p. 97.

4. Robert Caro, *Master of the Senate* (New York: Alfred A. Knopf, 2002), p. 95.

5. Mary Dalrymple, "Byrd's Beloved Chamber Deaf to His Pleas for Delayed Vote," *CQ Weekly*, October 12, 2002, p. 2674.

6. Walter J. Oleszek, *Congressional Procedures and the Policy Process, Seventh Edition* (Washington: CQ Press, 2007), p. 1.

21. QUORUMS

1. Seth Lipsky, *The Citizens Constitution* (New York: Basic Books, 2009), p. 27.

22. INTRODUCING LEGISLATION

1. Committee on House Administration, "The Bill Status System for the United States House of Representatives," July 1, 1975, p. 19.

23. HOLDS AND FILIBUSTERS

1. *Congressional Record*, June 1, 1989, S5939.

2. Walter J. Oleszek, interview with the author, December 9, 2011.

3. Ibid.

4. "Marathon Nomination Debate Reprises Familiar Partisan Refrains," by Jennifer A. Dlouhy and Adam Graham-Silverman, *CQ Today*, November 13, 2003, Updated 3:01 p.m.

5. "Marathon in the Senate: The Talk is Long, but Temper Short," by Neil A. Lewis, *New York Times*, November 14, 2003. p. A14.

24. MOVING LEGISLATION

1. Donald Ritchie, *The U.S. Congress, a Very Short Introduction* (New York: Oxford, 2010). pp. 20–21.

25. THE POLITICS OF INCLUSION

1. Howard Baker Leader's Lecture, July 14, 1998, Washington, D.C.

26. LEADING *AND* REPRESENTING

1. Gerald Ford, Leader's Lecture, May 23, 2001, Washington, D.C.

27. BUILDING COALITIONS

1. Walter J. Oleszek, *Congressional Procedures and the Policy Process, Seventh Edition* (Washington: CQ Press, 2007), p. 19.

2. Doris Kearns Goodwin, *Lyndon Johnson and the American Dream* (New York: Harper and Row, 1971), p. 11.

3. Senator Tom Daschle with Michael D'Orso, *Like No Other Time* (New York: Crown Publishers, 2003), p. 97.

4. Donald Ritchie, interview with the author, August 5, 2011. Washington, D.C. Tape-recorded.

5. Ibid.

28. LOBBYISTS

1. "Durbin, Tester, lobbyists, and the Dodd-Frank corruption machine," by Timothy P. Carney, *San Francisco Examiner,* June 14, 2011.

2. Donald Ritchie, *The U.S. Congress: A Very Short Introduction* (New York: Oxford, 2010), p.

3. Paul Simon, *P.S., the Autobiography of Paul Simon* (Chicago: Bonus Books, 1999), p. 306.

4. H. Johnson and D. S. Broder, *The System: The American Way of Politics at the Breaking Point* (Back Bay Books, 1997), pp. 213–214.

30. FLOOR ACTION

1. Walter J. Oleszek, *Congressional Procedures and the Policy Process, Seventh Edition* (Washington: CQ, Press, 2007), p. 226.

2. Ibid., p. 210.

32. THE YEAS AND NAYS

1. Bob Dole, Leader's Lecture, March 28, 2010. Washington, D.C.

33. "THE THIRD HOUSE OF CONGRESS"

1. Walter J. Oleszek, *Congressional Procedures and the Policy Process, Seventh Edition* (Washington: CQ Press, 2007), p. 16.

34. VETOES AND OVERRIDES

1. Bob Dole, Leader's Lecture, March 28, 2010. Washington, D.C.

2. Senator Tom Daschle with Michael D'Orso, *Like No Other Time* (New York: Crown Publishers, 2003), p. 217.

35. THE FEDERAL BUDGET PROCESS

1. Howard Baker, Leader's Lecture, July 14, 1998, Washington, D.C.

2. "Tempers flare as debt-limit deadline nears," by David Jackson and Mimi Hall, *USA Today*, July 14, 2011.

3. "S&P downgrades U.S. credit rating," by Charles Riley, *CNN .com*, August 6, 2011.

37. LEGISLATIVE OVERSIGHT AND INVESTIGATIONS

1. Walter Mondale Leader's Lecture, September 4, 2002. Washington, D.C.

38. NOMINATIONS—ADVICE AND CONSENT

1. Senator Tom Daschle with David Nather, *Getting It Done*, (New York: Thomas Dunne Books, 2010), pp. 118–121.

2. "Senate GOP Filibusters Obama Judicial Nominee," by Sunlen Miller, *ABC News.com*, December 6, 2011.

3. Jim Abrams, Associated Press, January 27, 2011.

4. *The Supreme Court: A C-SPAN Book Featuring the Justices in their Own Words,* edited by Brian Lamb, Susan Swain and Mark Farkas (Philadelphia: Public Affairs, 2010), p. 6.

39. IMPEACHMENT

1. "Samuel Chase," PBS, *An American Experience*, online.

40. DECLARING WAR

1. George H. W. Bush, Leader's Lecture, January 20, 1999, Washington, D.C.

2. Senator Tom Daschle with Michael D'Orso, *Like No Other Time* (New York: Crown Publishers, 2003), p. 123.

41. TREATIES

1. Robert Caro, *Master of the Senate* (New York: Alfred A. Knopf, 2002), p. 40.

2. Ibid., p. 44.

42. BUSINESS ON A HANDSHAKE

1. George H. W. Bush Leader's Lecture, January 20, 1999, Washington, D.C.

2. Robert Dole Leader's Lecture, March 28, 2010. Washington, D.C.

43. PRESS AND PRESSURES

1. David Donald, *Lincoln* (New York: Simon and Schuster, 1995), p. 233.

2. Donald R. Matthews, *U.S. Senators and Their World* (New York: W. W. Norton & Company, 1973), p. 203.

45. TECHNOLOGY

1. Robert Caro, *Master of the Senate* (New York: Alfred A. Knopf, 2002), p. 3.

2. Walter J. Oleszek, interview with the author, December 9, 2011.

46. WOMEN IN THE SENATE

1. "A Gillibrand Campaign: More Women in Politics," by Raymond Hernandez, *New York Times,* July 4, 2011.

2. Donald Ritchie, interview with the author, August 5, 2011. Washington, D.C. Tape-recorded.

3. Times Topics—People: Barbara A. Mikulski, *New York Times,* updated January 5, 2011.

48. SECURITY

1. Donald Ritchie, interview with the author, August 5, 2011. Washington, D.C. Tape-recorded.

50. ESCALATING PARTISANSHIP

1. Gerald Ford, Leader's Lecture, May 23, 2001, Washington, D.C.

2. Richard A. Baker, *200 Notable Days*, GPO, Washington, 2006, p. 94.

3. Senator Tom Daschle with Michael D'Orso, *Like No Other Time* (New York: Crown Publishers, 2003), p. 94.

51. THE SENATE'S SLIDE

1. Ledyard King, "Conservatives tout Noem as 'star of the future'," *Argus Leader*, February 11, 2011.

2. Walter Mondale, Leader's Lecture, September 4, 2002. Washington, D.C.

52. THE PRICE OF PARTISAN GRIDLOCK

1. Frank Lautenberg, *Congressional Record*, March 25, 1994, S4025.

53. THE FUTURE

1. Howard Baker, Leader's Lecture, July 14, 1998, Washington, D.C.

2. David McCullough, *John Adams* (New York: Simon and Schuster, 2001), p. 23.

INDEX